VISIBLE SAINTS

The History of a Puritan Idea

VISIBLE SAINTS

The History of a Puritan Idea

BY

Edmund S. Morgan

NEW YORK UNIVERSITY PRESS

1963

FOR

Perry Miller

ANSON G. PHELPS LECTURESHIP ON EARLY
AMERICAN HISTORY

PREFACE

FROM THE TIME they stepped ashore at Plymouth and Salem, the New England Puritans have commanded attention, partly because of the boldness of their undertaking, partly because of its material success, but also because of the tension, excitement, and hope aroused by a large-scale effort to deal rationally with society. Their attempt to direct human relations into a consistent pattern derived from Biblical precepts has been the focus of my own interest in the Puritans. In previous works I have discussed their concepts of family relationships and of civil government. Currently I am engaged in a study of the way their ideas affected economic problems. In the ensuing pages I have tried to examine the origins and history of an idea that they considered more important for society than domestic, political, or economic ones, the idea of membership in the church.

I owe an apology to Geoffrey Nuttall for adopting a title similar to that of his excellent book on English Congregationalism.[1] My excuse must be that what Mr. Nuttall says about the term "visible saints" is as true of the New England Congregationalists as of the English: the term "occurs repeatedly in their writings, was undoubtedly their controlling idea and

1. *Visible Saints: The Congregational Way, 1640–1660* (Oxford, 1957).

provides the key to an understanding of what they were after." [2] It is this particular Congregational idea that I am wholly concerned with. I do not pretend, however, to have dealt with it exhaustively. This book originated as the Anson G. Phelps Lectures, delivered at New York University in February and March, 1962. I have somewhat expanded the four lectures in turning them into chapters and have added a brief concluding chapter, but the focus of the book remains, as in the lectures, on the early history of the idea. I have only sketched its history in New England after 1662, and I have scarcely touched its history in England after the founding of New England.

Mr. Nuttall is one of many scholars on whose writings I have depended. I hope I have made good use of them, especially the work of the man to whom this book is dedicated, who has carried the understanding of Puritanism to a level unattained in any other branch of intellectual history. Without his work and the encouragement he has always given me, I could not have attempted this study.

I owe more immediate debts to those who read the manuscript and offered criticisms. My wife, Helen M. Morgan, who has worked with me as always, is responsible for whatever clarity of thought and expression they may display. David D. Hall brought to my attention a number of documents which have figured largely in my presentation; and he and Sydney Ahlstrom saved me from many errors. George Langdon, Gay Little, Robert Middlekauff, and Norman Pettit have also been very helpful with both substantive and stylistic suggestions. It is only fair to say that the book still retains some statements with which my friends may disagree.

Finally I should like to express my admiration and gratitude for the two great book collections in which I have done my research. The first is Henry Martyn Dexter's collection of

2. *Ibid.,* p. viii.

Puritan tracts, preserved and steadily added to in the Yale University Library. The very existence of this collection is a challenge to scholarship. The second is a work of twentieth-century book collecting that dwarfs all previous efforts in the field: that of Clifford K. Shipton and the American Antiquarian Society in preparing microtexts of all the titles in Charles Evans's *American Bibliography*. Only those who have done research in early American history both before and after this undertaking began can appreciate the extent of its service to scholarship.

Edmund S. Morgan

CONTENTS

VISIBLE SAINTS

The History of a Puritan Idea

The Ideal of a Pure Church

※※

CHRISTIANITY teaches that God is good and man is bad, that God is in fact so good and man so bad that man deserves eternal damnation. Christians accordingly strive to overcome the imperfections that invite damnation. They seek to share the righteousness of Christ, and they join with other men in institutions designed to control and alleviate the effects of human corruption. In particular they join with other Christians in the institution which God Himself has prescribed for those who wish to approach Him, the church.

In managing their churches, Christians have inevitably been troubled by the very human badness they seek to overcome. "Corruption — too much corruption in these matters" is the perennial cry of church reformers, appalled at the impurities that men have introduced into God's temple.[1] Practices and beliefs, accumulating over the years, appear on fresh examination to be contrary to God's commands. And sometimes the church seems to be corrupted in its very matter: it seems to have admitted the wrong people to membership. In every age some re-

1. The quotation is from the *Second Admonition to Parliament*, *1572*, in W. H. Frere and C. E. Douglas, *Puritan Manifestoes* (London, 1907), p. 110.

formers have attacked not only corrupt forms of worship and organization but corrupt membership: they have sought to exclude wicked men and women from the church.

To exclude the wicked from the earliest Christian churches seemed at first an easy task. The wicked readily identified and excluded themselves from an organization that brought suffering and persecution to its members. By the very desire to join the early church, a man demonstrated a palpable devotion to the true faith. But St. Paul found the church at Corinth filled with unworthy members, and more and more, as Christianity won acceptance, men and women of unsaintly temper knocked at the doors of the church, and those who stood at the entrance had to decide whether or not to admit them. Since Christianity taught that all men are sinful in some measure, it was not easy to draw the line between good and bad, and the guardians of the church, recognizing that none was perfect, swept all but the most hardened sinners inside.

In reaction against this comprehensive policy, the first reformers seceded and set up churches of their own, from which, blind to the sin of their own complacency, they excluded anyone whom they considered less than perfect in his dedication to Christ. Although there were many different groups with as many different definitions of perfection — Montanists, Novatianists, Cathari — the group known as Donatists won the greatest notoriety and became for after ages the symbol of those who thought that the church of Christ could achieve in this world a holiness "without spot and wrinkle." [2]

In answer to the Donatists St. Augustine developed the

2. Thomas Long, *The History of the Donatists* (London, 1677), p. 10. Cf. George Gifford, *A Short Treatise against the Donatists of England, whome we call Brownists* (London, 1590). Actually, of

theory of the church which was to guide orthodox Christian thought on the subject. There were, according to Augustine, two churches. One was pure but invisible; it included every person living, dead, or yet to be born, whom God had predestined for salvation. The other was visible but not entirely pure; it included only living persons who professed to believe in Christianity. Not every member of the visible church was destined for salvation, for not every man who professed belief would actually possess the true belief, the saving faith necessary for redemption. The visible church, operating in the world of time and of human corruption, must inevitably contain sinful men. It was holy, but not completely so, not without many spots and wrinkles.[3]

Although the visible church must thus remain impure, Augustine acknowledged that it should strive for purity by excluding obvious and gross sinners, at least until they visibly repented. Subsequent generations, while disclaiming the Donatist ideal of perfection in this world, did make an effort to restrict church membership according to Augustine's formula. They tried also by means of instruction, admonition, and expulsion and by imposing penance for sins, to maintain the purity of those already admitted to the church. But reformers often found the efforts insufficient, and finally in the Reformation of the sixteenth century a host of zealous men left the established church to build new ones of their own. They left for different reasons, some because they disliked the ceremonies or the doctrines or the officers of the church, some because they thought its membership too indiscriminate. And as they differed in their discontents, so also in their

course, later generations attributed to the Donatists a greater perfectionism than they possessed.

3. G. G. Willis, *Saint Augustine and the Donatist Controversy* (London, 1950).

methods of reconstruction: some sought the help of kings and princes to reorganize the church on a national scale; others disclaimed assistance from any quarter and sought the kingdom of God in free associations of believers. These volunteers, whatever their doctrines, were usually dismissed by the others as Anabaptists, because some of them rebaptized themselves, maintaining that their baptism in the Catholic church had been false or that only adult believers should be baptized.

The Anabaptists held stricter views of church membership than most other reformers, so strict that the others charged them with Donatism, that is, with seeking a church of perfect purity in this world. This charge was also leveled against the most ardent reformers in England, the Puritans. Actually, the English Puritans were neither Anabaptists nor Donatists: they believed neither in rebaptism nor in perfect purity. But some of them did develop a unique conception of church membership, designed to make the visible church a closer approximation of the invisible than St. Augustine probably had in mind. How this conception originated and developed in England, Holland, and New England is the subject of this book.

The Reformation in England, though it may have had popular roots in the Lollard movement of the fifteenth century, did not begin officially until the 1530's when Henry VIII repudiated the pope. Henry's object in freeing England from Rome was to free himself from Catharine of Aragon and to strengthen his own authority.

4. *The Seconde Parte of a Register,* ed. Albert Peel (2 vols.; London, 1915), I, 96.

Since he had few aspirations toward purity, either personal or ecclesiastical, he did his best to keep his popeless church otherwise unchanged and un-Protestant. But the ideas of the great continental reformers spread rapidly in a country that had formally rejected Rome. Moreover, Henry allowed the translation of the Bible into English, and the Bible became in England, as on the continent, a measure by which to judge the departure of the church from God's prescriptions. English reformers multiplied, and at the accession of Henry's ten-year-old son, Edward VI, in 1547, they gained a controlling influence at court. Under Edward, "that blessed ympe," as a later reformer called him, the English church was stripped of many Roman ceremonies.[4] Edward's sister Mary the reformers considered a different kind of imp. When she ascended the throne in 1553 and handed England back to Rome, the most outspoken Protestants who escaped execution fled to the continent. There they learned more reforms from Calvin and from the Rhineland disciples of Zwingli and Bucer.[5] And there they gained experience in the founding and management of churches of their own.

Upon Mary's death and the accession of Elizabeth in 1558, the English exiles returned to their own country to resume the work they had started under Edward. But Elizabeth was no child. She felt competent to run England and the English church without direction either from ardent papists or ardent Protestants. After making bishops of the most moderate reformers she could find, she allowed a return to most of the practices of Edward's day and had them established formally in the Thirty-nine Articles of 1563. But she stubbornly and skillfully resisted

5. The influence of Rhineland reformers on the Marian exiles is emphasized in L. J. Trinterud, "The Origins of Puritanism," *Church History*, XX (1951), 37–57.

further reforms and the dissatisfied extremists, who wanted to eliminate every relic of Romanism, were derided as Puritans, a term designed to suggest that they were Donatists. In spite of Elizabeth's political skill, the Puritans increased their numbers steadily and continued to demand further reforms. But by the close of Elizabeth's reign they had made little headway. In the year 1600 a Puritan listed ninety-one things still wrong with the Church of England.[6] Among other offenses, he objected to the use of the Apocrypha, to liturgies and set forms of prayers, to prohibitions of marriage and of eating meat at certain times, to the rituals used in baptism, in the Lord's Supper, in marriages and burials; he objected to confirmation, to popish vestments, to the neglect of preaching, to tithes, canon law, bishop's courts, and to the very existence of archbishops, lord bishops, and some thirty-odd other offices recognized by the church.

In every Puritan catalogue of corruptions, unscriptural ceremonies and offices occupied the largest place; but Puritans also found corruption in the membership of the church: in the men and women who belonged to it and received its sacraments, and in the men who occupied its offices. In attacking the membership of the church, the earliest Puritans assailed the clergy more often than they did the laity. Many of the English clergy had held positions in the Roman church under Mary and had made no public repentance of their sins for so doing. Though the Puritans did not maintain that a reversion to popery was unpardonable, they did think that unrepentant Catholic priests were unfit to be Protestant ministers. Moreover, for lack of other pliable candidates, Elizabeth's new

6. Francis Johnson, *An Answer to Maister H. Jacob his Defence of the Churches and Ministery of England* ([*Middelburg*], 1600), pp. 63-66. Johnson was a Separatist and might have repudiated the term "Puritan." I use the word to cover all who thought the Elizabethan

bishops had filled vacant benefices with incompetent and disreputable men, unqualified to preach the gospel while able but intransigent Puritan preachers were rejected and silenced.

Puritans set much store by preaching, which they considered the principal means ordained by God for instructing people in the great truths revealed by the Scriptures. A thorough understanding of those truths was necessary to salvation, and Puritans therefore resented the appointment of ministers who were unable or unfit to instruct their congregations by preaching. In petitions, admonitions, and supplications to Parliament, Puritans complained of the "Dumme Doggs, Unskilful sacrificing priestes, Destroyeing Drones, or rather Caterpillars of the Word," who occupied the pulpits of England.[7] Puritans thought that a minister must be learned in the Scriptures in order to bring understanding to others. In England, they said, too many ministers substituted an affected eloquence for sound knowledge and indulged themselves "in fonde fables to make their hearers laughe, or in ostentation of learning of their Latin, their Greke, their Hebrue tongue, and of their great reading of antiquities."[8]

Worse than these dilettante preachers were the ignorant and evil ministers, incapable of preaching at all, "some having bene Shoemakers, Barbers, Tailers, even waterbearers, shepheards, and horse keepers."[9] And lest the Parliament think these accusations rash, Puritans compiled lists of the unpreaching and unworthy ministers in various counties, with names of witnesses to support the unflattering descriptions of them. Among those in Essex County, for example, in 1586, were the following:

settlement to be not sufficiently reformed.
7. *Seconde Parte of a Register*, II, 211.
8. Frere and Douglas, *Puritan Manifestoes*, p. 110.
9. *Seconde Parte of a Register*, II, 77.

Mr Levit, parson of Leden Roding, a notorious swearer, a dicer, a carder, a hawker and hunter, a verie careles person, he had a childe by a maid since he was instituted and inducted. . . .

Mr Vawx, vicar of High Ester, a verie negligent man, and one that spendeth much time at the bowles, cards, and tables, and one verie careles for his familie, for his wife and children want at home while he spendeth abroad.

James Allen, vicar of Shopland, some time a serving man, unable to preach, for he cannot render an accompt of his faith, neither in Latine nor English, yet made a minister within these 3 or 4 yeeres.

Mr Phippe, vicar of Barling, Sometime a sadler by occupation, convicted of whoredome, who kept a whore long time in his house, a man far unable to preach.

Mr Atkins, curate of Romford, thrice presented for a drunkard.

Mr Palmer, parson of Widford, heretofore a servingman or a souldier, a gamster and pot companion, he received into his house a strumpet, who was brought to bed there, which was done to save her from punishment, himself was called before the spirituall court for the same; he allso usuallie marieth unknowne persons without anie banes.

Mr Hailes, vicar of Witham, n[o] p[reacher], one that gave a summe of money to two men to conceile his pretensed whoredoome at Islington, and so there promised that he would never inveigh against adulterie while he lived, which vow he hath hitherto kept.

Mr Ampleforth, vicar of Much Badow hadde a childe by his owne sister, and it doth appeare to be true by his diverse examinations, and deposition taken as well before Justices of Peace as in the spirituall court before the high commissioners, as allso by keeping of the child in sundrie places at his charges; he is also suspected of poperie, sometime a popish priest, and he is one that doth falsifie the Scriptures.

Mr Goldringe, parson of Laingdon Hills, he was convicted of fornication, a drunkard.

Mr Cuckson, vicar of linsell, unable to preach, hee hath bene a pilferer, of scandalous life.

Mr Mason, parson of Rawrey, had a childe by his maide, and is vehementlie suspected to have lived incontinentlie with others, and was brought for the same before a Justice of peace.[10]

With such men for ministers the Puritans foresaw that the membership of the Church of England could never be anything but ignorant, degraded, and corrupt. Without good teachers to instruct them, how could Englishmen recover from the dark ages when Rome had kept them in ignorance of the Scriptures? Puritans complained that even after fifty years of reformation "the greatest part of the people of the land, are altogether blinde and ignorant of true religion: yea more ignorant than is credible to any, that hath made no trial of us, as though we had neuer dwelt within the listes of Christendome." [11] And with the people as with their ministers, ignorance went hand-in-hand with wickedness. "Goe to Alehouses," charged the Puritans, "on the Sabboth dayes, there is as well solde all kinde of loosenesse as victuals. Goe to Greenes, there is myrth that would wound a Christian mans heart with heauinesse. Go to Fayres, there is a shew and trafficke, as well of all lewdnesse, as of wares." [12]

Inside the churches on a Sabbath one found mostly men

10. *Ibid.*, pp. 157–62.
11. *A Parte of a Register* [Edinburgh, 1593], p. 305.
12. *Ibid.*, p. 289.

and women unworthy of Christ, whose participation in the sacraments defiled the other members and profaned the ordinance: "what a pitifull thing is it, to come into a congregation of one or two thousand soules, and not to finde aboue foure or fiue that are able to giue an account of their faith in any tollerable manner, whereby it may be said probably: *This is a Christian man, or hee is a childe of the Church.*" [13] According to the Book of Common Prayer, which prescribed the order of church services, ministers were supposed to exclude notorious and unrepentant evildoers from communion; but where a minister was himself evil and unrepentant, he was scarcely qualified or likely to carry out this trust. Consequently men were thrust "in their sinne to the Lordes Supper." [14]

It was plain to the Puritans that the visible church in England stood too far from the invisible; it indiscriminately embraced the flagrantly wicked along with the good or sincerely repentant. According to the Scriptures as the Puritans read them, God had provided a means for cleansing the church of evildoers, whether members or officers. The church was to have no temporal powers, no authority to punish by fine or imprisonment, but it was to exercise discipline over its members by admonishing or censuring anyone who committed a sin and failed to repent. If the admonition brought no repentance, then the church was to excommunicate the offender, in other words cast him out. The Puritans believed that the power of excommunication, along with lesser disciplinary powers, belonged of right to individual churches and their ministers; but in the Church of England, as in that of

---

13. *Ibid.*, p. 305.
14. Frere and Douglas, *Puritan Manifestoes*, p. 14.
15. John Robinson, *Works*, ed. Robert Ashton (3 vols.; Boston, 1851), II, 60.
16. Frere and Douglas, *Puritan Manifestoes*, p. 106. For other Puritan statements of the importance of discipline and its abuse in the Church

Rome, the bishops claimed all disciplinary powers and denied them to the churches. The churches were therefore unable to rid themselves of unworthy members. Nor could they count on the bishops to help them; for the bishops' courts, as John Robinson said, played with excommunication like a child with a rattle: notorious thieves and adulterers went scot free, while honest men were excommunicated for trifles and could get the sentence lifted only by paying exorbitant fines.[15] Everything was done, said one Puritan, for "mistress money." [16]

Thus the absence of proper discipline in the church was doubly grievous: it violated God's commands in the Scriptures, and it prevented the reformation of other evils. The bishops by clinging to their courts and failing to use them against real offenders made purification of the church impossible. No wonder, then, that the bishops should be resented: as renegades, as holders of unwarranted offices, as appointers of wicked clergymen, and as obstacles to reformation. "You are in league with hell, and have made a covenant with death," John Udall told them in 1588.[17] And the bishops proved it by having Udall sentenced to death.

At this time Puritans were agreed on the main outlines of the church they wished to substitute for the bishops' league with hell: all church officers should be elected by the church to which they ministered; each church should have a pastor, a teacher, ruling elders, deacons, perhaps widows, and no other officers; no church

of England, see *ibid.*, pp. 33–34; *Seconde Parte of a Register*, I, 64–66, 132, 164–71, 197, and II, 54; Bertrand de Loque, *A Treatise of the Church* (London, 1581), pp. 234–58.

17. John Udall, *A Demonstration of the truth of that Discipline, which Christ hath prescribed in His Word, for the government of his Church, in all times and places, until the end of the world*, ed. Edward Arber (London, 1880), p. 6.

or minister should be subordinate to another but all should
be joined in brotherly communion in some kind of association. And finally, what is most important for our
purposes, they agreed that every church should exclude
and expel the wicked.[18]

With so large an area of agreement about the nature
and organization of the church, disagreements were confined to details; and as long as Puritans remained powerless to establish the desired organization, details could not
be important. Only after the calling of the Long Parliament in 1641 had brought the Puritans into control of
the English government and enabled them to proceed
with reform, did details of organization have to be decided. Then some Puritans preferred to leave each individual church independent of outside control, while others
thought that the ministers of the churches should be organized into presbyteries, consociations, and synods in
order to enforce orthodoxy among themselves. Those
who held the latter view became known as Presbyterians;
those who held the former were called Independents or
Congregationalists. By the time the names were attached,
the two groups had also diverged in their views of church
membership though both would have excluded from the
sacraments many of those whom the Anglican church
admitted.

I mention these later divisions here only because historians have commonly projected them back into the

18. See the references in note 16. The lack of clear differentiation
between Presbyterians and Independents or Congregationalists in the
sixteenth century is exemplified by John Udall. Udall has generally
been regarded as Presbyterian, but he apparently attempted to practice
something very close to what would later have been called Congregationalism, for he was charged with gathering a group for worship,
whom he called the children of God and who refused "to mix with
others, and many of them accompanied him to London, and com-
municated privately there." In defending himself, Udall said that "If
any have been led by his sermons to separate themselves from sinners,

period with which we are presently concerned, the sixteenth century. It is my own impression that with the exception of a very small minority, to be noted shortly, few Puritans identified themselves as Presbyterian or Independent before the 1640's. Until then, the differences between the two were seldom discussed and have often been exaggerated. Even in the early 1640's it is difficult to apply the labels with any certainty, for men acknowledged to be Independents turn up everywhere in the Presbyterian organization established by the Puritan Parliament.[19] It is possible to detect individuals who lived and wrote in the sixteenth and early seventeenth centuries as leaning either toward Independency or toward Presbyterianism — William Perkins, for instance, looks like a Presbyterian, William Ames like an Independent — but neither called himself such and both were revered by all Puritans. Since the Puritans themselves were not much concerned about the Presbyterian or Congregational aspects of Puritanism before the exodus to America, their differences need not concern us further in this chapter.

The fact is that before the disputes of the 1640's, virtually all Puritans agreed on certain basic principles of church organization and on the basic nature of the church. They would certainly all have accepted the definition of a church given by John Field in 1572. Field was

they have done well and obeyed St. Paul." *Seconde Parte of a Register,* II, 39–48.

19. J. H. Hexter, "The Problem of the Presbyterian Independents," *Reappraisals in History* (Evanston, Ill., 1961), pp. 163–84. Raymond P. Stearns, *Congregationalism in the Dutch Netherlands* (Chicago, 1940) emphasizes conflicts between Presbyterians and Congregationalists in the English churches in Holland, but after the death of John Robinson, most of his congregation joined the Scottish (presumably Presbyterian) church of Hugh Goodyear in Leyden. See D. Plooij, *The Pilgrim Fathers from a Dutch Point of View* (New York, 1932). The latest historian of English Congregationalism, Geoffrey Nuttall, maintains that Congregationalism did not really begin there until the 1640's. *Visible Saints: The Congregational Way, 1640–1660* (Oxford, 1957), pp. 8–14.

perhaps the foremost early Puritan leader, the author of the Admonition to Parliament of 1572, in which Puritan demands were first clearly articulated. Field, probably writing from Newgate prison, defined a church as "a company or congregatione of the faythfull called and gathered out of the worlde by the preachinge of the Gospell, who followinge and embraceinge true religione, do in one unitie of Spirite strengthen and comforte one another, dayelie growinge and increasinge in true faythe, framinge their lyves, governmente, orders and ceremonies accordinge to the worde of God." [20] This conception of the church as a group of believers "gathered out of the world," set apart from the wicked, would have been acceptable to Puritans whether Presbyterian or Congregational, whether in England or America, whether in 1572 or 1672. This was the church that Puritans were trying to make a reality as the sixteenth century drew to a close.

But while all agreed on the end to be sought, not all agreed on the means of reaching it. After Elizabeth had ascended the throne and disappointed Puritan hopes that her government would at once arrange for the establishment of proper churches, the great majority of Puritans had concentrated on achieving power and support within the government. They sought seats in the House of Commons and became the most vocal and powerful group in Parliament. They even won a few places on the Queen's Council.[21]

At the same time they tried to sway the government

20. *Seconde Parte of a Register*, I, 86.
21. M. M. Knappen, *Tudor Puritanism* (Chicago, 1938); J. E. Neale, *The Elizabethan House of Commons* (London, 1949), pp. 40–41, 241, 251–54; *Elizabeth I and Her Parliaments* (2 vols.; London, 1953, 1957), *passim*.
22. *Seconde Parte of a Register*, I, 89.

by means of the most appropriate and potent weapon at their disposal, the press. If words could have won the day for them, surely they would have succeeded, for in an age of eloquence the Puritans were persistently, pointedly, and painfully eloquent. They published a stream of books, pamphlets, and admonitions to Queen, Parliament, and bishops in words that grew more stinging as time passed. When chided for their lack of charity, they would reply, as John Field did in 1572, "We have used gentle words to[o] long, and we perceive they have done no good. The wound groweth desperate, and dead flesh hath overgrowne all, and therefore the wound had neede of a sharp corsive and eatinge plaister. It is no tyme to blanch, nor to sewe cushens under mens elbowes, or to flatter them in their synnes." [22]

Though often addressed to the authorities of church and state, the Puritan writings were clearly intended also for popular consumption. Public opinion did not yet play as important a role in government as it did a few decades later; but the Puritans nevertheless exerted themselves to capture public sympathy, for they believed that every government originates in popular consent and ultimately depends on popular support.[23] As Field is reported to have said at one time, "Seeing we cannot compass these things by Suit nor Dispute, it is the Multitude and People that must bring them to pass." [24] And a torrent of pamphlets sought to enlist the people on the side of reform.

But neither Field nor any other Puritan in pamphlet or

23. These views received their fullest articulation in the pamphlets justifying tyrannicide during the reign of Mary: Christopher Goodman, *How Superior Powers Oght to be Obeyd* (Geneva, 1558); John Knox, *The First Blast of the Trumpet against the Monstrous Regiment of Women* (1558); John Ponet, *A Shorte Treatise of Politike Pouuer* [London, 1556].

24. *Seconde Parte of a Register*, I, 15.

speech appealed to the people in order to overthrow the government. Though Puritans had not hesitated to make such an appeal against the government of Mary, they all remained loyal in a sense to the church whose reform they sought. Their aim was to gain control of the existing government and through the government to reform the church.

While the majority of Puritans thus looked to the government as the likeliest avenue by which to reach their goal, a small minority took a more direct route. These men, although loyal to the existing government, had decided that government action was neither a possible nor an appropriate means to reform the church, that indeed the English church, like the Roman, was beyond reform. The thing to do, they believed, was to begin at once to organize new churches from which the ignorant and wicked would be excluded. To do so would defy the laws of the realm and invite persecution by the government. But Puritans had faced persecution before and had even set up churches of their own before. The Protestants who fled to the continent during Mary's reign had organized churches at Frankfurt and Geneva and Wittenberg; and some of those who remained in England had secretly formed churches there and had met regularly to hear the word preached and to receive the sacraments.

After the accession of Elizabeth the churches abroad and the clandestine ones at home had dissolved in the expectation of reform in the Church of England. When that expectation failed, it was only natural to think of reviving

25. *Parte of a Register,* p. 25.
26. Albert Peel, *The First Congregational Churches* (Cambridge, 1920); Champlin Burrage, *The Early English Disenters in the Light of Recent Research* (2 vols., Cambridge, 1912), I, 80–94; II, 13.
27. Henry M. Dexter, *The Congregationalism of the Last Three Hundred Years as Seen in Its Literature* (New York, 1880), pp. 61–128; *The England and Holland of the Pilgrims* (London, 1906), pp. 188–99; Williston Walker, *The Creeds and Platforms of Congregation-*

them. Thus one group in London, finding the Anglican ceremonies too much to bear, remembered, as one of their members testified in 1567, "that there was a congregation of us in this Citie in Queen Maries dayes: And a Congregation at *Geneva*, which used a booke and order of preaching, ministering of the Sacraments and Discipline, most agreeable to the worde of God." [25] This group, and another led by one Richard Fitz, seem to have met as churches at Plumbers Hall in London in the late 1560's.[26]

Subsequently, about 1580, a group was formed under Robert Browne at Norwich.[27] Browne was the first to defend publicly the act of separating from the Church of England, and Puritans who carried out his recommendations are generally known today as Separatists. In a tract called *Reformation without Tarrying for any*, he decried the idea of waiting for the government to reform the church.[28] Though he professed complete subjection to civil authority, he denied that Christians could wait for government orders before worshiping God in the way that God demanded, that is, in churches that excluded wicked members and unscriptural ceremonies and offices: "the kingdom off God was not to be begun by whole parishes," Browne declared, "but rather off the worthiest, were they never so fewe." [29] Although Browne later recanted and was therefore repudiated by subsequent Separatists, his name became attached to them. They called themselves brethren of the separation, but everyone else at the time called them Brownists.

It is impossible to know how many Separatist (Brown-

alism (New York, 1893), pp. 1–27.

28. [Middelburg, 1582].

29. *A True and Short Declaration, both of the Gathering and Joyning Together of Certaine Persons* [1584], p. 6. I have used an unidentified nineteenth-century reprint in the Dexter Collection, Yale University Library, corrected against the unique original by Henry M. Dexter.

ist) churches were formed in England during the reign of
Elizabeth, but it seems likely that the numbers were small,
the persons humble in circumstance, and the total membership under a thousand.[30] Besides the Plumbers Hall
churches and Browne's church at Norwich, part of which
moved to Middelburg in Holland in 1581, there was a
church formed in London in the 1580's or early 1590's
under Henry Barrow and John Greenwood, who were
executed for it in 1593. Their church continued under the
ministry of Francis Johnson and moved to Amsterdam to
escape further persecution. Other Separatists followed. In
1606 members of a church originally formed at Gains-
borough in Lincolnshire arrived in Amsterdam under the
leadership of John Smyth, and in 1610 a dispute in the
first church resulted in the formation of a third under
Henry Ainsworth. Holland also became the refuge of the
famous band of Separatists from Scrooby. Led by John
Robinson, this group came to Amsterdam in 1607, settled
in Leyden in 1609, and in 1620 furnished the founders of
the first permanent settlement in New England at Plymouth.[31]

Though few in numbers, the Separatists were im-
mensely important in furthering the development of
Puritan ideas about the church. In the very act of separating and in running their churches, free from control by
the Anglican hierarchy, they were obliged to make de-

30. Burrage, *Early English Dissenters*, I, 152; Peel, *First Congregational Churches*, pp. 44–45.

31. Dexter, *England and Holland of the Pilgrims*, pp. 199–595; F. J.
Powicke, *Henry Barrow* (London, 1900).

32. *An Arrow against the Separation of the Brownists* (Amsterdam,
1618), p. 93.

33. *An Answer to John Robinson of Leyden by a Puritan Friend*,
ed. Champlin Burrage (Cambridge, Mass., 1920), p. 74. Cf. *Seconde
Parte of a Register*, I, 72.

34. For evidence of such a practice, see Robinson, *Works*, II, 101;

cisions and to think out the implications of Puritan principles before other Puritans did.

It must be admitted that the Puritans who remained within the Church of England were sometimes able in some localities to practice some of the doctrines that they professed. A few churches owned the right to choose their own minister; and where a patron in control of a benefice became a Puritan, he could allow the church to elect the minister and then appoint the man they elected. The Reverend John Paget wrote concerning his ministry at Nantwich, "notwithstanding the license and allowance which I had from the Bishop, yet did the substance of my calling consist in the free and generall consent of the people who being publiquely assembled together, did then choose me to be a teacher unto them." [32] And one anonymous Puritan defended on similar grounds the church of which John Robinson had been pastor before he became a Separatist. This was St. Andrew's in Norwich, where the minister was "freelye chosen by the congregacyon not by the patron nor by the Bishop . . . the confirmacyon of the Bishop denyes not free election to the people." [33] Puritan ministers could and did omit ceremonies and vestments when no known pursuivants or agents of the bishops were at hand. In running his church, a Puritan minister might even select a special group of worthy people and debar all others from the sacraments.[34] But

John Smyth, *Parallels, Censures, Observations* ([Amsterdam], 1609), p. 4; Henry Ainsworth, *Counterpoyson Considerations* ([Amsterdam], 1608), pp. 231–32; John Cotton, *The Way of the Congregational Churches Cleared* (London, 1648), p. 20; *Some Unpublished Correspondence of the Reverend Richard Baxter and the Reverend John Eliot*, ed. F. J. Powicke (Manchester, 1931), pp. 24–25; T. M. Harris, *Memorials of the First Church in Dorchester* (Boston, 1830), pp. 53–57; W. W. Biggs, "The Controversy concerning free Admission to the Lord's Supper, 1652–1660," Congregational Historical Society, *Transactions*, XVI (1949–1951), 178–89, at p. 185.

none of these halfway measures could be practiced consistently or confidently; no Puritan within the Church of England could pursue the implications of his principles the way the Separatists did. It took time and experience to work out the full meaning of each doctrine, to fix its relationship to other doctrines, and to devise institutional forms for embodying it in practice.

The Separatists learned the implications of their ideas not only by practicing them but by defending them against attacks. Like other Puritans they had an extraordinary confidence in the fruitfulness of argument, and through their arguments, spread before the world in print, we can discern the ways in which they applied and developed the Puritan conception of the church as a company of faithful people, gathered from the world. The Separatists defended themselves not only against the Anglicans but more particularly against their fellow Puritans who remained in the Church of England. These nonseparating Puritans repudiated those who left the church and argued that it was the duty of all Christians to support and sustain any church of which they were members. They insisted that no church could be perfect, that the mere existence of errors in a church was not sufficient reason for leaving it. To leave a church, however corrupted by the inevitable sinfulness of man, was schism and schism was always wrong. But the Separatists denied the charge of schism: they had not separated from another church. Their decision to separate was a decision that the Church of England was no church at all.

The Separatists defended this decision on two grounds: first, that the Church of England lacked what they con-

35. *Institutes of the Christian Religion*, trans. John Allen (Philadelphia, 1932), II, 220–47.

sidered an essential quality of a church, namely discipline, the power to rid itself of unworthy members; second, that it had not been founded in the proper manner by the proper people and hence had never actually been a church.

In maintaining the first of these charges, the Separatists had no difficulty in demonstrating that the English churches lacked the power of discipline. This fact was readily admitted by most of their opponents. What they had to prove was that discipline was essential to the existence of a church. In affirming this principle, the Separatists went a step beyond the continental reformers from whom Puritan ideas were derived. John Calvin, for example, though he had described the use of admonition and excommunication to rid the church of unworthy members, at the same time had emphasized that the essential marks of a church were the preaching of the word and the administration of the sacraments. Where these existed, even in the absence of discipline, Calvin said, a church existed, and separation was schism.[35] Calvin followed Augustine in deploring the ambition of the Donatists who sought a church free from every spot. And he likewise belabored the Anabaptists who confined church membership to freely professing adult believers. Calvin saw the Anabaptists as modern counterparts of the Donatists, who thought it possible to make the visible church identical with the invisible. These men, he said, "from a false notion of perfect sanctity, as if they were already become disembodied spirits, despised the society of all men in whom they could discover any remains of human infirmity."[36] Everyone should understand, Calvin main-

36. *Ibid.*, p. 234.

tained, that the visible church must be "composed of good and bad men mingled together" [37] and the failure to correct faults by discipline was no cause for withdrawal. The ministry of the word and administration of the sacraments "have too much influence in preserving the unity of the Church, to admit of its being destroyed by the guilt of a few impious men." [38]

The notorious failure of discipline in the English churches led most Puritans to lay a somewhat heavier stress on it than Calvin did,[39] but most Puritans agreed that discipline though highly desirable was not absolutely necessary to the existence of a church. John Field again stated the majority view that "thoughe there be many faults in our churches, such as are not to be impudentlie defended, but with speede by ordenarie meanes to be mended, as lacke of Discipline and a righte governmente of the Churche," yet the English churches would remain true churches "so long as open defiance is not bidd to Christians, but that they maie injoye the truthe of doctrine in the most substantiall poincts, and have the Sacraments in diverse places ministred according to our Saviour Christes institutione." [40]

The Separatists thought that it took more than the preaching of true doctrine and the administration of the sacraments to make a church. If a church did not have the power to correct its own faults by discipline, it was not a church. They were not, they hastened to say, perfection-

37. *Ibid.*, p. 235.
38. *Ibid.*, p. 238.
39. One Puritan criticism of the Church of England's Thirty-nine Articles even questions "whether the 19th article do describe a visible Church sufficientlie enoughe, leaving out Discipline a necessarie marke therof." *Seconde Parte of a Register*, I, 197.
40. *Ibid.*, p. 86.
41. *An answere to Master Cartwright His Letter for Joyning with*

ists: they too despised the Donatists and the Anabaptists;
they too understood that the visible church could not be
spotless. They did not maintain, Robert Browne insisted,
that "we may be without sinne, or that the church may
be without publike offences, or if there fall out some sort
of grosser sinnes, that therefore it should cease to be the
church of God. We teach no such doctrine. . . ." [41]
What they did maintain was that a church must have the
power to correct itself by expelling the wicked. Therefore if any gross sins became incurable, "and the Church
hath not power to redresse them, or rebelliously refuseth
to redresse them, then it ceaseth to be the Church of
God." [42] Where discipline was wanting, Browne concluded, there was "no true shewe nor face of an outwarde
and visible Church of God." [43]

It remained for Henry Barrow, the fiercest spokesman
of the Separatist position, to repudiate John Calvin directly in the point of church discipline. Barrow, writing
from his prison room in the Fleet, where he awaited execution for his ideas, was ready to acknowledge that Calvin
was "a painful and profitable instrument [of God], in the
thinges he saw, and times he served in," but "being so
newly escaped out of the smoky fornace of poperie, he
could not so sodeinly see or attaine unto the perfect
beawtie of Sion." [44] What Calvin failed to see, Barrow
said, was that a church cannot exist without "either wil
or power to reforme and amend any default which is

the English Churches (London, [1583]), p. 32. Cf. Henry Barrow,
A Brief Discoverie of the False Church [Dort, 1590], p. 17; Francis
Johnson, *A Treatise of the Ministery of the Church of England* [1595],
p. 75; Ainsworth, *Counterpoyson*, pp. 178–79, 195; Walker, *Creeds and
Platforms*, p. 71.

42. *An answere to Cartwright*, p. 32.
43. *Ibid.*, p. 45.
44. Barrow, *Brief Discoverie*, p. 13.

committed amongst them." [45] Barrow made the usual de-
nunciation of "that damnable sect of the Anabaptistes,
which fantastically dreame unto themselves a Church in
this life without spot," [46] but he thought that Calvin in
his eagerness to refute the Anabaptists and "to defend his
owne rash and disorderly proceedings at Geneva" had
perverted the Scriptures and deceived his followers.[47] To
make preaching and the sacraments the distinguishing
criteria of a church and discipline a mere "hang-by" was
to speak in contradictions, for without discipline there
could be no proper administration of the sacraments to
those worthy to receive them.[48]

In condemning the rash and disorderly proceedings at
Geneva, Barrow was referring to Calvin's method of converting that city to Protestantism. Calvin, he said, "at the
first dash made no scruple to receave al the whole state,
even al the profane ignorant people into the bozome of
the Church, to administer the sacramentes unto them." [49]
This indiscriminate gathering of saints and sinners into a
supposed church had become, Barrow believed, "a misera-
ble president, and pernitious example, even unto all Europe, to fall into the like transgression." [50] And the
Church of England had fallen into this transgression when
it swept in papist and Protestant alike in the wholesale
conversion of the realm after Mary's death.[51] This was no

45. *Ibid.*, p. 18.
46. *Ibid.*, p. 33.
47. *Ibid.*, p. 33.
48. *Ibid.*, p. 26.
49. *Ibid.*, p. 33. Barrow was misinformed in supposing that Calvin
was so indiscriminate in founding the church at Geneva. Actually
Calvin debarred from communion all "qui se declairent et manifestent
par leur meschante et inique vie nappertenir nullement a Jesus." *Opera
Selecta*, eds. Peter Barth and William Niesel (5 vols.; Munich, 1926–
1952), I, 371.
50. Barrow, *Brief Discoverie*, p. 33.
51. "All this people . . . were in one daye, with the blast of Q.
Elizabeths trumpet, of ignorant papistes and grosse idolaters, made
faithfull Christianes. . . ." Barrow, *Brief Discoverie*, p. 10.

way to form a church; according to Barrow and Browne and all other Separatists, a church must originate as a voluntary association of persons worthy to worship God. It must contain only men who freely professed to believe, and tried to live according to, God's word. And it could not exist unless such men voluntarily agreed to join together for worship and voluntarily agreed to subject themselves to discipline. A church could not be formed by governmental compulsion or by constraint of the wicked, but only by free consent of the good.[52]

This then was the second ground of the Separatists' arguments that the Church of England was no church at all: it had not been founded in the proper manner by the proper people. Elizabeth had swept the whole people of England into her so-called church just as Calvin had allegedly done with the people of Geneva. Every Englishman had been automatically transformed by government decree into a member of the new Anglican church. There had been no voluntary gathering of believers.[53] There-

52. These ideas and those in the next two paragraphs were expressed at length in the writings of Robert Browne, Henry Barrow, Henry Ainsworth, John Robinson, John Smyth, and Francis Johnson. A convenient formulation of them is Ainsworth and Johnson, *A True Confession of the Faith* ([Amsterdam], 1596), reprinted in Walker, *Creeds and Platforms*, pp. 49–74.

53. "This people yet standing in this fearfull sinfull state [after the death of Mary] / in Idolatry / blyndnes / superstition / and all manner wickednes / without any professed repentance / and without the meanes theroff / namely the preaching off the word goeing before, were by force and aucthority of lawe onely compelled / and together received into the bosome / and body of the Church / their seed baptised / themselves received and compelled to the Lords supper / had this ministery and service (which now they use) injoyned and set over them / and ever synce they and their seed remayne in this estate / being all but one body commonly called the Church of England." *Certayne Letters translated into English, being first written in Latine* (1602), p. 8; *An Apologie or Defence of Such True Christians as are commonly (but uniustly) called Brownists* (1604), p. 8. This is a new preface written for the Confession of Faith of the Amsterdam church. Cf. Barrow, *Brief Discoverie*, p. 10; *A Collection of Certain Letters* ([Dort], 1590), pp. 4, 16, 20, 39, and *passim*; John Robinson, *Works*, I, 96–97, 316–17, 489; Ainsworth, *Counterpoyson*, pp. 127–51.

fore even if the government should someday reform the laxity of discipline and other corruptions in the Church of England, it would still not be a proper church.

There was in fact no way to reform the churches of England into the kind of churches that the Separatists found in the Bible except by starting all over again from below, as the Separatists were doing. Professing Christians must separate from the wicked and form true churches by voluntary agreements or covenants made among themselves. Without such a covenant there could be no church. Nor could there be a church encompassing a whole people, not only because it was inconceivable that all the people should be worthy of membership, but also because it was physically impossible for the whole people of a nation to gather together in one place. The covenant which formed a church must be subscribed to personally: the people's representatives in Parliament could not act for them in this matter; and though the covenant might include as few as two or three persons, it could not include more than could gather at a single place to worship together.[54] In other words, the only true churches were those which later became known as Congregational.

There was some disagreement among the Separatists as to whether the churches of England had ever been gathered by voluntary covenants in the approved manner.

54. Barrow, *Brief Discoverie*, pp. 12–13; Ainsworth, *Counterpoyson*, p. 136; Robinson, *Works*, II, 132. On church covenants, see Champlin Burrage, *The Church Covenant Idea* (Philadelphia, 1904).

55. Ainsworth, *Counterpoyson*, pp. 225–27; Robinson, *Works*, II, 127.

56. ". . . there was not one congregation separated in Queen Mary's days, that so remained in Queen Elizabeth's. The congregations were dissolved, and the persons in them bestowed themselves in their several parishes, where their livings and estates lay." Robinson, *Works*, II, 489.

57. Johnson, *A Treatise of the Ministery of England*, pp. 11, 104;

Some maintained that there might have been such covenants at the first conversion of English Christians from
paganism; others denied the possibility.[55] But all agreed
that if there ever had been true churches based on covenants in England, they had ceased to exist with the rise
of the papacy, and if any were founded subsequently,
they had certainly ceased under Mary, except for the
few clandestine churches founded by reformers, which
had dissolved with the accession of Elizabeth.[56]

The voluntary character of the association by which a
church was formed had many implications for the
Separatists. It led, for example, to their insistence that
each local congregation be independent of other congregations or of any higher church organization, and that
the ministry be supported by voluntary contributions and
not by tithes or by contributions from the civil government.[57] As a corollary of this view, the members of
Francis Johnson's Amsterdam church affirmed in 1596
that no true Christian should contribute anything to the
support of false ministers, i.e., those of the Church of England.[58]

In the conduct of worship as in the formation of their
churches, the Separatists stressed spontaneity. Following
the regular sermon of the minister, they set aside a time
for "prophecying," that is, little extempore sermons or
speeches by members of the congregation.[59] These in turn

Ainsworth, *Counterpoyson*, pp. 197–98; Robinson, *Works*, II, 466–67;
Smyth, *Paralleles*, p. 120; Walker, *Creeds and Platforms*, p. 79.
   58. Walker, *Creeds and Platforms*, p. 69.
   59. *The Examinations of Henry Barrowe, John Greenwood, and
John Penry* (London, [1662]), pp. 30–31; Smyth, *Paralleles*, pp. 63, 133;
Christopher Lawne *et al.*, *The Prophane Schisme of the Brownists or
Separatists* ([London], 1612), pp. 58–59; Robert Baillie, *A Dissuasive
from the Errours of the Time* (London, 1645), pp. 58–59; *Chronicles
of the Pilgrim Fathers*, ed. Alexander Young (Boston, 1841), pp. 419–22.

were followed by a period for questions from the congregation about any points in which the sermon or prophecying had left them in doubt.[60] They frowned on all set forms of prayers and liturgies, including the Lord's Prayer, which they regarded simply as a perfect example of a prayer, not as a set form of words to be repeated.[61] Both the election and the ordination of the minister were to be performed by the members of the church.[62] Marriages were not a church matter at all and were to be performed by a simple declaration in front of witnesses.[63]

The church led by John Smyth in Amsterdam carried the insistence on voluntarism and spontaneity in worship somewhat farther than other Separatists. Smyth and his church maintained that a minister must not even have the Bible or any other book open before him when preaching but must rely entirely upon the spontaneous utterances of his heart. The only assistance he might properly employ was to open a copy of the Old Testament in Hebrew or the New Testament in Greek — translations would not do — and having read a verse in the original tongue, close the book and proceed with his sermon. In singing psalms, the congregation was likewise to make no use of books.[64]

As Smyth and his congregation carried voluntarism farther than other Separatists, so Separatists in insisting on voluntary association in the first place, were only carrying an accepted Puritan principle farther than other Puritans — just as they had done in the case of church discipline.

60. Baillie, *Dissuasive*, p. 118.

61. Johnson, *A Treatise of the Ministery*, pp. 138–41; Walker, *Creeds and Platforms*, pp. 73–74.

62. Walker, *Creeds and Platforms*, pp. 25–26, 35, 66.

63. *Ibid.*, p. 79; Henry Barrow, *A Collection of Certaine Sclaunderous Articles* ([Dort], 1590), sig. G, f. ii; Paget, *An Arrow against the Separation of the Brownists*, p. 30.

64. John Smyth, *The Differences of the Churches of the seperation* (1608).

65. See references in note 23.

The Reformation had generated a powerful impulse toward free consent as the basis of both state and church. And while most reformers stopped short of a full acceptance of this principle, Puritans were committed to it, at least in broad terms. During the reign of Mary Tudor many, in affirming the right of tyrannicide, had maintained that government originates in a social compact.[65] By the beginning of the seventeenth century, an important group of nonseparating Puritan divines were affirming, almost in the words of the Separatists, that a church too must originate in a covenant among the members. Henry Jacob, for example, acknowledged in 1604 that a church is formed "by a free mutuall consent of Believers joyning and covenanting to live as Members of a holy Society togeather"[66] and in 1610 he defined a church as "a number of faithfull people joyned by their willing consent in a spirituall outward society or body politike, ordinarily comming together into one place, instituted by Christ in his New Testament, and having the power to exercise Ecclesiasticall government and all Gods other spirituall ordinances (the meanes of salvation) in and for it selfe immediatly from Christ."[67] Similarly William Ames, Paul Baynes, and William Bradshaw, who were not Separatists, maintained that a church can be no larger than a congregation and must originate in a voluntary conjunction of believers.[68]

Although many nonseparating Puritans accepted the

---

66. Burrage, *Early English Dissenters*, II, 157.

67. Henry Jacob, *The Divine Beginning and Institution of Christs true Visible or Ministeriall Church* (Leyden, 1610), sig. A, f. 1.

68. William Ames, *A Second Manuduction for Mr. Robinson* (1615), p. 33; *The Marrow of Sacred Divinity* in *Works* (London, 1643), ch. xxxii; Paul Baynes, *The Diocesans Tryall* (1621); William Bradshaw, *English Puritanisme* (1640), p. 6. On the acceptance of Congregational principles by nonseparating English Puritans, the classical works are Burrage, *Early English Dissenters;* and Perry Miller, *Orthodoxy in Massachusetts* (Cambridge, Mass., 1933), especially pp. 73–101.

principle that a church must rest on a covenant subscribed by believers, they were hard pressed to produce the covenant on which any existing English church was based. Indeed, there was much in the charge one Separatist made in 1611, when describing the differences between Separatists and other Puritans. "The former," he said, "doe both hold and practise the truth, and separate themselves from the contrarie. The latter have the truth in speculation onely and either dare not or at least doe not practise it." [69] Henry Jacob at first attempted to defend the Puritans' inconsistency; but later, perhaps as a result of some conversations he is known to have had with the Separatist pastor John Robinson, he gave up the argument and even joined in forming a church of his own by covenant in London in 1616. [70]

Other Puritans argued that the English churches rested on covenants which, though not explicitly subscribed or agreed to at any particular time or place, were nevertheless implicit. [71] To this the Separatists could answer, as Governor William Bradford did, that "such an Implised [covenant] as is Noe way explised is Noe better than a popish Impliced faith . . . and a meer fixion," or, he added, it is like "a Marriage Couenant which is noe way explissed." [72] In 1614 William Bradshaw tried to argue that the English churches, though formed by compulsion of the magistrate, rather than by voluntary association, might nevertheless in the course of time purify themselves and become true churches of believers "joined together

69. *Mr. Henry Barrowes Platform* (1611), p. 143. I have consulted this work in a transcript by Henry Martyn Dexter in the Yale University Library.

70. Jacob, *A Defence of the Churches and Ministrye of Englande* (Middelburg, 1599); Burrage, *Early English Dissenters*, II, 292–94.

71. Miller, *Orthodoxy in Massachusetts*, p. 87.

72. Colonial Society of Massachusetts, *Publications*, XXII (1920), 116–17.

in the fellowship of the Gospell by voluntarie profession of the faith, and obedience of Christ." [73] But Bradshaw did not explain precisely how this transformation could be accomplished, especially in the absence of proper discipline.

There was no getting around the fact that explicit church covenants and church discipline were both practical means of achieving the purer church that Puritans longed for, and no Puritan was able to suggest a better means. Because most Puritans accepted the premises from which the Separatists started, the Separatists in their arguments generally came off the better and thus gradually pushed their opponents toward their own conclusions.[74] Ames, Bradshaw, and Jacob, who were widely esteemed among English Puritans, accepted virtually all the Separatist principles except separation and thereby won for those principles a large following in England. That following, though unwilling to desert the Church of England, nevertheless shared with the Separatists the belief which underlay the Separatist practice of voluntary association and subjection to discipline: a church should rest on a covenant, voluntarily subscribed by believers, and should exclude or expel all known evildoers.

John Field's 1572 definition of the church had described it as "a company or congregatione of the faythfull called and gathered out of the worlde by the preachinge of the Gospell." A Separatist church was precisely that — a company of the faithful, gathered in a voluntary association

73. *The Unreasonableness of the Separation* (Dort, 1614), sig. P.
74. R. Alison, *A Plaine Confutation of a Treatise of Brownisme* (London, 1590), even argued (p. 126) that at the accession of Queen Elizabeth some of those who formed the new church were true believers and "There was therefore such a separation at her maiesties entrance unto the Crowne, as the visible Church in all ages from the beginning hath afforded." This refutation of Separatism thus acknowledged the principle of separation.

out of the world. The Separatists were practicing the principles which other Puritans held only in speculation, or as we would say, in theory. The Separatists had therefore to decide, long before other Puritans, a very troublesome question. If the church was a company of the faithful, who was indeed faithful? Who was worthy to join the company and who must be left out or cast out into the world? This question, which at first seemed simple, proved increasingly difficult to answer.

The Separatist Contribution

❦

PURITANS, whether they separated from the Church of England or not, never repudiated St. Augustine's distinction between the visible and the invisible church. They all insisted on the impossibility of a church without blemish in this world. But they all thought the English churches not pure enough, and the Separatists thought them too impure to bear the name of church.

Although part of the impurity the Separatists complained of lay in improper ceremonies and offices, their most persistently voiced criticism was that the Anglican church contained persons unfit to be members even of the visible church, persons who had never submitted voluntarily to the gospel and whose behavior advertised their indifference to God's commandments. Every Englishman, they complained, was by the mere fact of residence in a parish, a member of the parish church; and however ungodly his beliefs or behavior, the parish church was powerless to expel him.[1]

The Separatists withdrew from the Church of England in order to establish churches of their own in which the membership would more closely approximate that of the invisible church. But they could neither create nor main-

1. Robinson, *Works*, II, 96–97.

tain such churches without deciding who was or was not worthy of belonging to them. They therefore set up standards of membership by which to control both the admission of members and their continuance in the church.

Because Separatists were the first Puritans to establish such standards, because they were the first Puritans to practice what was later called Congregationalism, historians have assumed that the Separatists formulated all the principles by which later Congregationalists, after the founding of New England, tried to make their churches resemble the invisible church. These later Congregationalists, like the Separatists and like all other Puritans, began with the premise that human merit is negligible and that salvation depends entirely on saving faith, which cannot be attained by human effort but comes only from God's free grace. Or to put it another way: though no human deserved salvation, God in his mercy had chosen to save a few, and to them He gave saving faith. They belonged to his real, his invisible church. To make the visible church as much as possible like the invisible, the later Congregationalists argued that the visible church in admitting members should look for signs of saving faith. Granted that the signs would be fallible, for only God knew with certainty whom He had saved and whom He had not, the church should nevertheless try to form an estimate, try to assure itself of the probability of faith in every candidate it accepted. Men, being human, would make mistakes, and the visible church would therefore remain only an approximation of the invisible; but it should have in appearance the same purity that the invisible church had in reality: it should admit to membership only those who

2. See below, Chapter 3.
3. Walker, *Creeds and Platforms*, p. 33.

appeared to be saved, only those who could demonstrate by their lives, their beliefs, and their religious experiences that they apparently (to a charitable judgment) had received saving faith.

Such by the 1640's was the reasoning of Congregationalists both in England and in New England.[2] And it is plausible to assume that the Separatists, starting from the same premises about saving faith and the nature of the church, must have reasoned in the same way about the requirements for church membership. Did they? What qualifications did the Separatists, the first Congregationalists, actually establish as necessary for membership in the visible church?

The Separatists, in defining church membership, generally used the same language as other Puritans. The church was to be "a companie and fellowship of faithful and holie people."[3] The crucial question is what they meant by "faithful and holie." They answered in part by stating what they did not mean: outside the church were to be "dogs and Enchaunters, and Whoremongers, and Murderers, and Idolatours, and whosoever loveth and maketh lyes."[4] They answered also in indictments of the English parish churches or "mixed assemblies," as they insisted on calling them. They condemned these assemblies for "their generall irreligious profannes ignorance, Atheisme and Machevelisme on the one side, and publique Idolitrie, usuall blasphemie, swearing, lying, kylling, stealing, whoring, and all maner of impietie on the other side."[5] No one, they complained, was excluded from the Church of England, "be they never so prophane or wretched, no Atheist, adulterer, thief, or murderer, no lyer, perjured, witch or conjurer, etc. all are one fellow-

4. *Ibid.*, p. 40.
5. *Ibid.*, p. 51.

ship, one body, one Church." [6] John Greenwood, having stated that the church ought to exclude the profane, explained what he meant by that term: "Atheists, men without the knowledg or feare of God, together with the papists, hereticks, and all other infidells." [7]

Wicked behavior, ignorance of Christian doctrine, and heresy — these were the charges that the Separatists brought against the members of the parish assemblies. Nowhere did the Separatists charge that the English churches failed to inquire into the religious experiences of members in the effort to detect saving faith. Did they then mean that good behavior, knowledge of Christian doctrine, and lack of heresy were sufficient to qualify a man as faithful and holy? For a more explicit answer we must examine their own procedures, first for admitting members and second for expelling them.

Evidence for determining the Separatist admission procedures is scanty, especially for the earliest churches. The only requirement clearly demanded for membership in the first churches was assent to a covenant, that is, an agreement to join with the other members in the worship of God and obedience to His commandments. This agreement, in some churches at least, included a declaration explicitly rejecting the fellowship of the Anglican church.

In the first strictly Separatist church of which there is record, Richard Fitz's at Plumbers Hall in London, the covenant seems to have consisted entirely in repudiating the Anglican church and forswearing attendance at Anglican services. The only suggestion of a deeper commitment is in these words: "Inasmuch as by the workyng

6. *An Apologie or Defence*, p. 8.
7. Barrow, *A Collection of Certaine Sclaunderous Articles*, sig. C, f. i.

also of the Lorde Jesus his holy spirite, I have joyned in prayer, and hearyng Gods worde, with those that have not yelded to this idolatrouse trash, notwithstandyng the danger for not commyng to my parysh church &c. Therefore I come not back agayne to the preachynges &c. of them that have receaved these markes of the Romysh beast." [8] Here, though the Holy Spirit is mentioned, He is credited only with opening the applicant's eyes to the falsity of doctrines inherited from Rome. The crucial requirement for membership appears to have been repudiation of the English church.

Robert Browne's account of the formation of his church at Norwich has the same emphasis. All members were supposed "to forsake and denie all ungodliness and wicked fellowship and to refuse all ungodlie communion with wicked persons. For this is it that is most, and first of all needful, because God will receave none to communion and covenant with him which as yet are one with the wicked, or do openlie themselves transgresse his commaundements." [9] The covenant agreed to by the members, if we may trust Browne's account, was more extensive and explicit than any other of which there is record:

So a covenant was made and ther mutual consent was geven to hould together. There were certain chief pointes proved unto them by the scriptures, all which being particularlie rehersed unto them with exhortation, thei agreed upon them and pronounced their agrement to ech thing particularlie, saiing: to this we geve our consent.

First therefore thei gave their consent to joine them selves to the Lord in one covenant and felloweshipp together and

8. Burrage, *Early English Dissenters*, II, 13–15; Peel, *First Congregational Churches*, p. 37.

9. *True and Short Declaration*, p. 12.

to keep and seek agrement under his lawes and government; and therefore did utterlie flee and avoide such like disorders and wickednes as was mencioned before.[10]

Browne goes on to give the details of church procedures and order of worship agreed to by the company. Nowhere does he describe any effort by the church to search the religious experiences of the members. The evidence of holiness that Browne looked for lay in godly behavior and in shunning the company of the ungodly.

The only other sixteenth-century Separatist church of which we have a record was that of Barrow, Greenwood, and Johnson, formed about 1588 in London. One of the members of this church deposed in court in 1593, that at admission "he made this protestation that he wold walke with the rest; and that so longe as they did walke in the way of the Lorde, and as farr as might be warranted by the word of God." [11]

Such statements are the only surviving clues to the admission procedures of the first Separatist churches in England. There is no suggestion in any of them that the members were subjected to a test for determining their possession of saving faith. The only requirements stated or hinted at are that a candidate must be of godly behavior, must by a positive act join himself with the existing members, and must by a positive act sever his connections with the Church of England. But the statements are so brief that they may not reveal all the requirements for membership. In the absence of other evidence, we may

10. *Ibid.*, pp. 19–20.
11. Henry M. Dexter, *The Congregationalism of the Last Three Hundred Years as Seen in its Literature* (New York, 1880), p. 265n. Johnson had previously attempted to impose a convenant on a church of English merchants at Middelburg. See Burrage, *Church Covenant Idea,* pp. 49–50.

perhaps glean some further hints from the procedures of an earlier Puritan church at Frankfurt about which more is known. The Frankfurt church, which had been established in 1554 by Puritan exiles fleeing from the rule of Queen Mary, was Separatist only by circumstance; but later Separatists revered it as a precedent for their own churches.[12] The Frankfurt exiles had at the outset drawn up a platform of discipline "whereunto all those that were present subscribed / shewinge therby that they were ready and willing to submitt themselves to the same / accordinge to the rule prescribed in gods holie word / at which time it was determined by the congregation that all suche as shulde come after / shulde doo the like / befor they were admitted as members off that churche." [13]

The details of this platform are unknown, for the document itself has not survived; but a few years later, after a long and tedious dispute, the Frankfurt church successively adopted two more platforms, both of which were printed in an account of the dispute. Both agreed, substantially, on the requirements for admission, which the second one stated as follows:

Firste / for the auoidinge off all heresies and sectes in oure churches euery one as well men as wemen which desier to be receiued shall make a declaration / or confession off their faithe before the ministers and elders / shewinge him selff fully to consent and agree with the doctrine off the churche and submittinge them selues to the Discipline off the same / and the same to testifie by subscribing therto yf they can wryte.

12. George Johnson, *A Discourse of some troubles and excommunications in the banished English Church at Amsterdam* (Amsterdam, 1603), *passim.*

13. [William Whittingham], *A Brieff discours off the troubles begonne at Franckford in Germany Anno Domini 1554* ([Zurich], 1575), p. 8.

Item yff anye person so desyrous to be receyved into the congregation be notoriously defamed / or noted off any corrupt behaviour or evill opinion in doctrine / or slaunderous behaviour in liffe / the same maie not by the Ministers and Elders be admitted / till he haue either purged himselff theroff or ells haue declared himselff to the ministers and elders penitent for the same.[14]

According to this statement, the Frankfurt church (in what amounts to a covenant) seems to have required not merely submission to the church, with a promise of good behavior, but also a confession of faith. The meaning of this phrase is indicated by its context: a confession of faith was designed to prevent heresy, and it consisted of a statement of consent and agreement to the doctrines of the church. No explicit requirement of a confession of faith is mentioned in the surviving documents of the first Separatists in England; but the covenant of Robert Browne's church evidently included an agreement to the church's practices, and the later Separatist churches in Holland demanded that candidates agree not only to good behavior but also to the doctrines of the church.

After the execution of Henry Barrow and the removal of most of his church to Amsterdam, the members, under the pastorship of Francis Johnson, issued a statement of their doctrines, which they called *A True Confession of the Faith*. This asserted that no one was to be admitted to membership "but such as doo make confession of their faith, publickly desiring to bee received as members, and promising to walke in the obedience of Christ." [15] In 1598 another edition of the same document repeated in a new preface that "None of yeres may be received into the Churche without free professed fayth repentance and sub-

14. *Ibid.*, pp. 127–28.
15. Walker, *Creeds and Platforms*, p. 71.

mission unto the Gospell of Christ and his heavenly ordinances." [16] Henceforth one finds mention of a profession
or confession or declaration of faith in nearly every Separatist discussion of admission to church membership. In
some cases the covenant and profession of faith may have
been lumped together in one general statement. But in the
later churches the profession was not a part of the covenant, it was a distinct and separate requirement as John
Robinson, pastor of the Leyden church indicated, at least
obliquely, when he stated in 1610 that "the bare profession of faith makes not a true church, except the persons
so professing be united in the covenant and fellowship of
the gospel into particular congregations." [17]

A confession of faith or a creed had formed a standard
part of the order of worship in both the Anglican and the
Catholic churches, but the confession required of candidates in a Separatist church was not a ritual or a mere
memorized recital of a given text. The Separatists, like all
Puritans, emphasized the importance of knowledge and
understanding of Christian doctrine. They wanted a
church of believers, and they thought that belief without
knowledge and understanding was no belief at all. The
great offense of the Roman church had been to keep the
people ignorant; the continued offense of the Anglican
church was in appointing ignorant ministers and accept-
ing ignorant members. The Separatists' confession of faith
therefore involved not only a statement of the candidate's
acceptance of Christian doctrines but a demonstration of
his understanding of them. In the later churches and possibly in the earlier ones the ministers, elders, and members
questioned the candidate publicly in order to be sure that
he understood what he was saying when he made his con-

16. *Certayne Letters*, p. 8.
17. Robinson, *Works*, II, 480. Cf. Jacob, *Divine Beginning*, Preface.

fession or profession (the terms were used interchange-
ably).

Such a procedure, the Separatists insisted, bore no relation to the confession of faith that formed part of the
communion service in the Anglican church. The latter
was simply a creed, recited from the prayer book. On the
basis of it, Anglican ministers arguing with John Greenwood in 1590 had maintained that they admitted to communion only those who "make publike declaration of their
faith." Greenwood in answer had charged that the Anglican profession was meaningless, because it was merely
"the verball repeating certayne words taught them by
rote." Such a profession, he said, could be taught to a
parrot. He did not deny that a profession of faith should
precede the taking of communion, but it would be a
worthless profession, unless the man who made it did so
with a full understanding of what he was saying, an understanding that could come only from a good knowledge of
Christian doctrine. By Separatist standards few members
of the Church of England had such knowledge.[18]

A Separatist confession of faith, then, required both
understanding and belief. These, together with good behavior, constituted for the Separatists a sufficient proof of
the holiness and faith of prospective members. But the
Separatists, like other Puritans, must have recognized that
a man could attain understanding, belief, and good behavior without ever acquiring the saving faith that came
from God's election. As we shall see, when Congregational churches later attempted to test prospective members for saving faith, they continued to insist on a con-

18. Barrow, *A Collection of Certaine Sclaunderous Articles*, sig. C,
ff. i and ii. Cf. Johnson, *A Treatise of the Ministery*, p. 19; Ainsworth,
Counterpoyson, p. 63; Robinson, *Works*, II, 281–92.

19. "This is that faith which in schooles is called historicall, because
it goeth no further then to give assent and credit to the story of that

fession or profession of faith as a distinct and separate requirement. The faith implied in a confession of faith was not saving faith but simply an intellectual understanding of, and consent to, a set of doctrines; it was the product, not of grace but of instruction. To distinguish such faith from saving faith, Puritans often called it "general" or "historical" faith.[19] Saving faith must be preceded by historical faith, but historical faith was not necessarily followed by saving faith. Separatists doubtless assumed that a probability of salvation attended those who possessed historical faith and also obeyed God's commandments outwardly. But both these qualifications were within the grasp of human endeavor, and the Separatists looked no further in setting the standards of membership.

That the faith demanded by Separatists involved no more than understanding and consent is apparent in a revealing account of admission procedures that resulted from a quarrel in the first Amsterdam church between the pastor Francis Johnson and his brother George. In 1603 George published a lengthy narrative of the quarrel, which he compared to the famous one in the church at Frankfurt in the 1550's. In the comparison George Johnson discussed the practices of the Amsterdam church with regard to admissions, which he thought had deteriorated under the administration of his brother and of Daniel Studley, the ruling elder of the church. He began by stating the practice at Frankfurt, where, he said, "none / man or woman / were to be received members without making confession of their faith / also great care was in admitting youth to the supper of the Lord / none being

which God speaketh to be true, which one may beleeve for another; and therefore this cannot be true justifying faith, and this may be in those that knowe they are bidden to the wedding, yet refuse to come." Ezekiel Culverwell, *A Treatise of Faith* (London, 1623), p. 15. Cf. William Perkins, *Workes* (London, 1608–1631), I, 125; II, 207; III, 2.

to be admitted / til they were able to make confession of their faith before the whole congregation / and also to have an honest testimony of towardness in godly conversation." [20]

According to George Johnson these same standards had originally prevailed at Amsterdam, but "corruption creeping upon them, they now differ." The deterioration, he alleged, lay in the fact that the church no longer required a proper understanding in its candidates. Instead, the pastor and Daniel Studley admitted whom they pleased. If a candidate "can but say (yea) to that, which Daniel Studley speaketh, it is inough, he may be a member, though (if he be tried) he be not able to give account of any point of faith: if he confesse the English church to be a false Church promise to seperate frome it, and to walke with them, it is inough, though he know not what a false or true Church is, neither be able to render a reason forth of Gods worde, concerning a false or true Church: Whereas all Brethren ought to be redy to render a reason of the hope that is in them." [21]

The last statement might be thought to refer to saving faith, but in the context it is apparent that the church, before its deterioration, required an intellectual understanding and acceptance of certain doctrines, and that afterward it did not. George Johnson thought that Studley's procedures did not adequately test the candidate's understanding, but he did not say that anything more than understanding ought to be tested.

The understanding necessary for a confession of faith could be attained by every man who attended the preaching of the word. John Robinson, in discussing how civil government could support religion, suggested that magis-

---

20. *A Discourse of some troubles*, p. 78.   21. *Ibid*.
22. Robinson, *Works*, II, 315.

trates might require all persons under their jurisdiction to attend church and might even levy penalties on them "if after due teaching, they offer not themselves unto the church." [22] Robinson's words clearly imply that anyone who has heard the preaching of the gospel should be able to qualify himself for church membership and might be punished by the civil government if he failed to do so. Although Robinson may have said more than he intended, he certainly did not envisage saving faith as necessary for church membership. He would have affirmed without hesitation that saving faith is the free gift of God to a chosen few and unattainable by human instruction. And he would not have maintained that men who failed to receive saving faith should be punished in this world by the civil government.

Similarly John Smyth, minister of the Separatist church established in Amsterdam in 1606, described the qualifications for church membership in these three simple propositions:

> The way of receaving in of members is fayth testified by obedience.
> Fayth is the knowledg of the doctrine of salvation by Christ.
> Obedience is a godly, righteous and sober life.[23]

Here again the faith required for membership is simply knowledge of doctrine, not reception of supernatural saving grace.

Still another indication that Separatists did not demand evidence of saving faith lies in their manner of admitting children. The Separatists, like most Christians, Protestant

23. John Smyth, *Principles and inferences concerning the Visible Church* (1607), p. 13.

or Catholic, believed in infant baptism. Since baptism was the symbol of admission to the church, they therefore accepted children, provisionally at least, as members of the church. Only children whose parents or guardians were members received this privilege, but the child himself was not expected to display any sign of divine favor other than in his choice of parents. In order to be admitted to the Lord's Supper and the other privileges of adult membership, he must first grow old enough to "examine himself." When he felt that he had reached a belief and understanding of Christian doctrine and a reasonable ability to live in obedience to God's commandments, he demonstrated the fact to the church by making a profession of faith and assenting to the church covenant, and then he took his place at the Lord's Supper.[24]

There is no evidence that the profession which transformed a child member into an adult member involved any demonstration of saving faith, but there is again evidence of the necessity of understanding before professing. The ministers or elders of the church were expected to spend some time in weekly catechizing of the children in order to bring them to the necessary understanding, and the importance of this task is reflected in the fact that George Johnson accused his brother of neglecting it. George Johnson even suggested that Daniel Studley along with Henry Ainsworth wanted children admitted to the Lord's Supper before they were old enough for a proper understanding of the Christian religion. "Daniel Studley," he said, "and some other began to broche the error which had long lurked in M. Ainsworths bosome about the admitting of children to the supper of the Lord: But the Pastor (would God he had done in al things, as in that)

24. Walker, *Creeds and Platforms*, pp. 70–71; Johnson, *A Discourse of some troubles*, p. 111.

stopped it, and nipped the head in the hatching." [25] The Amsterdam church was thus saved from the heresy of offering communion to the ignorant.

Neither George Johnson nor any other Separatist suggested that the church demand anything more of its grown children than it demanded of outsiders seeking admission: understanding and acceptance of the truths of Christianity, good behavior, and voluntary submission to the discipline of the church. These were the terms of admission, and they lay within the grasp of every child born in the church and instructed by its officers and within the grasp of every man who attended the preaching of the word and tried to live accordingly. Although the Separatists considered saving faith necessary for entrance into the invisible church they did not attempt to discern it in those they admitted to the visible church, for saving faith was not within everyone's grasp. It was the free gift of God. Saving faith lay in the heart, where only God could see it; the visible church could not and should not examine the hearts of its members.

In the exercise of church discipline, as in the admission procedures, the Separatists concerned themselves with outward, visible behavior and with openly expressed opinions, not with the presence or absence of saving faith. The records of the Separatist churches, if any were kept, have not survived, but several cases of church discipline resulted in disputes in which each side took its case to the public in print. From the arguments we can gather more specific information about the offenses which made a man unworthy of membership, and we can learn something of

25. Johnson, *A Discourse of some troubles,* p. 79.

the way discipline operated. In the evidence I have examined there is no example of excommunication or admonition for any alleged absence of saving grace. In every case the ground for expulsion from the church was heresy or misconduct.

Probably the most notorious case of discipline involved Tomasine, the wife of Francis Johnson, who, as pastor of the Separatist church of London and Amsterdam, has already figured in our narrative. Mrs. Johnson had been the widow of a merchant, and she possessed a wardrobe that struck some of the church members, and especially the pastor's brother George, as immodest. George Johnson's accusations against Tomasine were titillating, more so perhaps than her actual garments were. He condemned:

First the wearing of a long busk [corset] after the fashion of the world. . . . 2. Wearing of the long white brest after the fashion of yong dames, and so low she wore it, as the world call them kodpeece brests. . . . 3. Whalebones in the bodies of peticotes . . . against nature, being as the Phisitians affirme hinderers of conceiving or procreating children. . . . 4. Great sleeves sett out with whalebones, which the world call . . . . . [This was so shocking a word that George Johnson could not bring himself to write it.] 5. Excesse of lace upon them after the fashion of yong Marchants wives Contrary to the rules of modesty. 6. Foure or five gould Rings on at once. . . . 7. A copple crowned hatt with a twined band, as yong Marchants wives, and yong Dames use. Immodest and toyish in a Pastors wife. . . . 8. Tucked aprons, like round hose. . . . 9. Excesse in rufs, laune coives, muske, and such like things. . . . 10. The painted Hipocritical brest, shewing as if there were some special workes, and in truth nothing but a shadow. Contrary to modesty, and sobriety. 11. Bodies tied to the peticote with points, as men do their dublets to their hose. . . . 12. Some also reporte that she laid forth her heare also. . . .[26]

26. *Ibid.*, pp. 135–36.

George Johnson did not contend that these garments and fashions were wicked in themselves, but that they were improper for the wife of a pastor, especially a pastor who was in prison, as Francis Johnson was at the time he married and for some time thereafter. George also found Mrs. Johnson's behavior below standard:

First she stoode gazing, bracing or vaunting in shop doores. Contrary to the rules of modest behaviour in the daughters of Zion. . . . 2. She so quaffed wine, that a papist in their company said to another woman: You leave some, and shew modesty, but Mrs. Johnson, shee etc. shee doth not. . . . 3. She laide in bedd on the Lordes day till 9 a clock, and hindered the exercise of the worde, she being not sick, nor having any just cause to lie so long.[27]

In dealing with this troublesome lady, George Johnson followed the approved procedure for a member who learned of an offense by another member: he remonstrated with her personally and alone in order to persuade her of her fault, and when this failed, he brought two other members to join him in reproving her. When this too had no effect, he took the matter up before the church and applied to her the third verse of the third chapter of Jeremiah: "Therefore the showers have been withholden, and there hath been no latter rain; and thou hadst a whore's forehead, thou refusedst to be ashamed." Francis Johnson responded to the accusations by insisting that his wife's clothes were perfectly proper and that, besides, they were none of his brother's business. Indeed, Francis Johnson, seconded by the ruling elder, Daniel Studley, charged George Johnson with uncharitableness and "overcarriage," a Puritan term for excessive zeal.

The quarrel had begun while both brothers were in prison for their beliefs in London. They were released in

27. *Ibid.*, p. 136.

1597 on condition that they leave the realm. They did so with the help of a ship captain, Charles Leigh, who was apparently a member of the church and Mrs. Johnson's cousin. Leigh took the Johnson brothers, together with Daniel Studley and another member, one John Clark, on an exploring expedition to Newfoundland and the Magdalen Islands.[28] During the voyage the quarrel between the brothers broke out again, and it continued through shipwreck, return to England, and exile to Amsterdam. It lasted for eight years and ended only with the excommunication not of the pastor's wife but of George Johnson and of John Johnson, the father of the disputants, who took George's side. George wrote an account of the whole affair in which he demonstrated his brother's numerous departures from proper church practices; but nowhere in all of the 217 closely printed pages did he suggest that the church ought to survey or attempt to determine the presence or absence of saving faith in its members. Nowhere did he imply that any member, once admitted, should be expelled for any reason other than heretical beliefs or bad behavior. The whole quarrel revolved around externals.

After George Johnson's expulsion in 1604 for slandering the pastor's wife, Francis Johnson and Daniel Studley evidently continued to expand their own authority, and the behavior of Studley became so outrageous that it offended even Henry Ainsworth, who previously had sided with Studley and Johnson in their dispute with brother George. Finally, in 1610, Ainsworth and a number of other members split from the church and formed a new one. When this occurred, according to a later renegade Separatist, the two groups excommunicated each other.[29]

28. *Ibid.*, pp. 106-13. The voyage is described in Richard Hakluyt, *Voyages* (London and New York, 1907), VI, 100-13.
29. Lawne *et al.*, *Prophane Schisme*, p. 42.
30. Henry Ainsworth, *An Animadversion to Mr. Richard Clyftons*

In subsequent years, if we may believe their opponents, Francis Johnson and Daniel Studley exercised tyrannical powers over the church and at the same time neglected to discipline real offenders. Johnson fell into the heresy of maintaining that the Roman Catholic Church was a true church, a position that is difficult to reconcile with Separatism at all; [30] and Studley was accused of what we would call sadism, and also of being too friendly with his maid, with his second wife's daughter, and with another church member named Mary Maie. Mrs. Maie was herself a cause of scandal. Besides singing bawdy songs, she was said to have been "in a whore-house upon some occasion, and creeping thence out at a window in a very untoward manner, was excused by *Dan. Studley*, who alledged in her defence the example of *Paul*, that by the Disciples was out a window, through the wall of Damascus, let downe by a rope in a basket." [31] In his own defense Studley did not attempt to deny his partiality for the three women, but he did argue somewhat abjectly that all his unchaste efforts with them had been unsuccessful.[32]

While Johnson's church thus fell a prey to heresy and to bad officers and lax discipline, the Separatist churches generally suffered from too free rather than too sparing use of excommunication. They cast out members not only for attending services in Anglican churches but also for marrying outside the church. In cases of adultery, where the wronged party was willing to forgive, the church refused to forgive unless the offender publicly expressed his repentance before the church. If he failed to do so, the church would cast out not merely the offender but the forgiving husband or wife too, thus in effect forbidding

Advertisement (Amsterdam, 1613), pp. 67–110; *A Reply to a Pretended Christian Plea for the AntiChristian Church of Rome* (1620).

31. Lawne *et al.*, *Prophane Schisme*, p. 25.

32. Richard Clyfton, *An Advertisement concerning a book lately published by Christopher Lawne* (1612), pp. 115–25.

charity and requiring a divorce as a condition of continued membership for the offended party.[33] So assiduous were the Separatists in their exercise of discipline that they finally found themselves maintaining that the failure to punish a single known offense was sufficient to destroy a church.[34]

This preoccupation of the Separatists with the outward behavior of members did not escape the attention of their opponents, who reminded them that ultimately it was not a man's behavior that mattered, but whether or not he had faith. Thomas Cartwright, a nonseparating Puritan, argued that nothing was necessary for a church except men with faith and that since the Anglican church did contain some who had faith it was a true church. In support of this argument Cartwright cited St. Paul's designation of the church as simply a company of the faithful. Robert Browne responded that though Paul spoke of the faithful without mentioning their works, "yet must we understande their fayth shewed by an outwarde good profession." [35] And though Christ had said judge not that ye be not judged, "wee are not thereby forbidden to examine the outwarde abuses and faultes of others." [36] Robert Browne would never have denied that faith was essential to salvation. But because his pamphlet concentrated on justifying the Separatists' concern with behavior while Cartwright concentrated on the importance of faith, Browne seemed to be in the unenviable position, for a Protestant, of minimizing faith and emphasizing good works.

33. Paget, *An Arrow against the Separation,* pp. 30–31.
34. Smyth, *Paralleles,* p. 70.
35. *An answere to Cartwright,* p. 41.
36. *Ibid.* Cf. Robinson, *Works,* II, 281–92.
37. Stephen Bredwell, *The Rasing of the Foundations of Brownisme*

Stephen Bredwell charged Browne with taking "the high way to Popery," of making good works rather than faith the essential quality of a church.[37] From here, said Bredwell, it was only a step to making good works the basis of salvation. George Gifford accused the Separatists of having already taken that step. In a pamphlet entitled *a Short Treatise against the Donatists of England, whome we call Brownists,* Gifford asserted that the Brownists, by their insistence on the necessity of punishing every sin, "make the stablenesse of Gods covenant, not to depend upon mercie and free grace promised and bound with an oth, but uppon our works. . . ." [38]

Gifford's turn of the argument must have seemed perverse and unfair to the Separatists. They had been talking about the qualifications not for salvation but for membership in the visible church. They had always acknowledged that there might be some of God's elect, possessing true saving faith, within the Anglican church and indeed within the Roman Catholic Church.[39] But neither the presence of such individuals nor the fact that they had received saving faith through the preaching of Anglican or Catholic priests, was enough to make the Anglican or Catholic churches true churches. A church, the Separatists insisted, must be composed entirely of persons who understood and accepted the doctrines of Christianity, submitted voluntarily to the church, and led lives free of apparent sin. And the church must have power to admonish or expel those who fell into open sin. As for inner, saving faith, only God could discern it; men could judge one another only by visible behavior.[40]

(London, 1588), pp. 44, 72, 92–96.

38. (London, 1590), p. 66.

39. Ainsworth, *An Animadversion*, p. 97; *Reply to a Pretended Christian Plea*, pp. 7, 99.

40. Robinson, *Works*, II, 486; III, 428.

As far as the visible church was concerned the Separatists were indeed preoccupied with behavior, with good works rather than saving faith. But in pressing their arguments, they were gradually, almost insensibly, led to interpret their definition of the church and their procedures for admission in such a way as to give more emphasis to saving faith. From the beginning they had presumed that the qualifications they demanded would produce a company of faithful and holy people. In gathering their companies, however, they had been more concerned to escape the palpable wickedness of the parish assemblies than to discover signs of divine grace. It was holiness in action that they looked for. But in defending themselves against the charge of neglecting faith, they could scarcely, as Protestants, maintain that good works were important in themselves. Robert Browne, while insisting on good behavior, had spoken of it as an evidence of faith, and by the end of the first decade of the seventeenth century, Separatists were placing more and more emphasis on the idea that their membership qualifications were signs of faith.

The leading figure in this reinterpretation was Henry Ainsworth, probably the most learned of all Separatists. As Anglicans and nonseparating Puritans continued to press the claim that the Anglican church was a true church because it brought saving faith to some, at least, of its members, Ainsworth launched a rebuttal that gave new meaning to the Separatist definition of the church. Separatist members, he said, already had faith, while the Anglicans' claim that they produced faith was in itself proof that the Anglican church was improperly constituted, because the members should have had faith before

41. *Counterpoyson*, p. 69.
42. *Counterpoyson*, p. 64.

they were admitted. The Scriptures, he argued, require "that people must be regenerate and born agayn, before they may be admitted into any particular church." [41] Regeneration by almost any definition, and certainly by any Puritan one, was the result of saving faith. Ainsworth was thus demanding that the church be composed of persons who had already received saving faith.

In keeping with this demand, Ainsworth interpreted the covenant that formed a Separatist church not simply as an agreement among a group of believers, but as an agreement in which God or Christ participated as well. He could now retort to the Anglicans and nonseparating Puritans "Your church can shew no covenant that was made between Christ and her, at any time: the gathering and planting of your church having been by the Magistrates authority; not by the word of Christ, winning mens soules unto his faith, separating them from the unbeleevers, and taking them to communion with himself." [42] In making God or Christ a party to the church covenant Ainsworth was following the old Separatist practice of taking an idea shared by other Puritans and pushing it into fresh territory. English Puritan divines were at this time developing a concept which they called the covenant of grace.[43] A covenant of grace, they said, existed between God and every man who had saving faith. The church covenant, Ainsworth implied, parallelled the covenant of grace, the one being between God and a saved individual, the other between God and a group of presumably saved individuals. That Ainsworth thought of church members as having saving faith he suggested again in his definition of a church: "every people called of God into covenant and communion with Christ, and one with an other, and so

43. Perry Miller, "The Marrow of Puritan Divinity," in *Errand into the Wilderness* (Cambridge, Mass., 1956), pp. 48–98; *The New England Mind: the Seventeenth Century* (New York, 1939), pp. 365–97.

walking, though with much weaknes, ignorance, and dayly syn; is to be estemed a true church of God: but they that are not so called and come into covenant with the Lord, howsoever they may professe many excellent truthes, yet want they the mayn essential thing which makes a true church." [44]

As he reinterpreted the covenants of the Separatist churches, Ainsworth also reinterpreted the confession of faith that was required for membership. The confession, in his view, implied the presence of saving faith: "Unto the church are to be admitted," he said, "all unto whom the covenant and promise of God doth apperteyn; and they are so many as the Lord our God shall call; and all those are called (in the judgement of man,) which having heard the word of God, doe professe repentance from dead works and faith in God, by Jesus Christ the alone Saviour of the world, and promise obedience to the word, through the holy Ghost the sanctifier of the elect." [45] In this definition the profession of faith is somewhat more than intellectual understanding and acceptance. An evaluation of the applicant's chances of salvation is clearly implied. By 1620 Ainsworth was condemning the creed and confession of faith which the Roman Catholics used as "but an assent to the trueth of Gods promises; and not a confidence of their justification [i.e., their salvation] in particular." [46] Ainsworth's complaint against the Catholic confession thus went well beyond Henry Barrow's earlier complaint against the Anglican one. Barrow had charged simply that the Anglican confession did not require real understanding; Ainsworth said that the Catholic confes-

44. *Counterpoyson*, p. 124.
45. *Counterpoyson*, p. 122.

sion did not require individual confidence of salvation, that is, saving faith.

John Robinson, the pastor of the Pilgrim church at Leyden, seems in some measure to have shared Ainsworth's new emphasis on faith. Though Robinson, as we have seen, at one point implied that anyone was capable of qualifying himself for church membership, he also maintained in the same tract that a true profession of faith could be made only by persons "visibly, and so far as men in charity could judge, justified, sanctified, and entitled to the promises of salvation, and life eternal." [47] But for Robinson a judgment rendered in charity would treat a man as entitled to salvation if his profession of faith was accompanied by outward good behavior.

Although Robinson and Ainsworth attached a new spiritual significance to the covenant and the profession of faith, it is unlikely that either man altered the procedures for admission to the church that had been established earlier. One of Robinson's opponents charged in 1609 that in spite of Separatist claims to a purer membership than the Anglicans, "yet you require but a voluntarye profession of covenant, which hipocrites maie make." [48] And Ainsworth himself maintained that the only way of testing faith was by behavior and profession. It was beyond human capacity to probe further. In arguing with the Anglicans about whether their church contained any regenerate members, Ainsworth told them plainly: *"Faith* is in the hart, . . . The hart no man knoweth but God alone. . . . So then I ask you how you know that your members have *true faith;* Your answer must needs be, (unlesse you

46. *Reply to a Pretended Christian Plea*, p. 9.
47. Robinson, *Works*, II, 332.
48. *An Answer to John Robinson*, p. 24.

wil make your self a God,) you know it not but by their words and works. Wel then, let us bring these to the trial; their *confession* and their *practise:* leaving their *faith* to God that knowes it." [49]

So far as can be ascertained, Ainsworth abided by this judgment. There is no evidence that either he or Robinson instituted any procedures for admission that looked beyond the individual's own assertion in his confession of faith, his subscription to the covenant, and his outward good behavior.

This, then, was the state of Separatist thought and practice when the *Mayflower* sailed to establish the first Separatist church and the first permanent English settlement in New England. The church was a company of the faithful, and faith may have meant something more than mere belief in the truths of Christianity. But so far as can be known, no procedures had been developed to test a candidate's heart for saving faith. The only ostensible requirements for admission to the church were a profession of faith, subscription to the covenant, and good behavior.

The Pilgrims, who carried these ideas and practices to the New World, were only a part of John Robinson's Leyden church. When they decided to leave Holland, a majority of the church voted to stay behind, probably with the intention of coming over later if the venture proved successful. Pastor Robinson remained with the majority in Holland; William Brewster, the ruling elder, accompanied the Pilgrims. Robinson died in 1625, and the Pilgrim church remained without a minister until 1629. Brewster preached regularly every Sunday, and other

49. *Counterpoyson*, pp. 62–63.
50. William Bradford, *History of Plymouth Plantation, 1620–1647,*

members "prophesyed," but Brewster as ruling elder was not qualified to administer the sacraments and he was not offered, or would not accept, the higher office of pastor or teacher.[50]

During this period when the church existed without a regular minister, the members could comfort themselves with Robinson's previously declared insistence that churches made ministers, not vice versa, and that a church could exist and could both admit and expel members without a minister.[51] A supply of candidates for admission was available from the men and women, not members of the Leyden church, who accompanied the Pilgrims and continued to arrive every year. In admitting new members from this group the Plymouth church probably followed the same procedures as the Leyden church, for it seems unlikely that the Pilgrims would have felt justified, without ministerial guidance, in developing new procedures. Unfortunately no formal records of the church survive for the first forty years of its existence in the New World, and we can determine its practices only from Governor William Bradford's famous history and from later recollections and controversial writings.

Bradford in two places described the admission of members to the Plymouth church during the first decade. The first involved John Lyford, who came to the colony in 1623. Lyford, who had been a clergyman in England, was expected to become a minister of the church. Of his admission Bradford says: "After some short time he desired to joyne him selfe a member to the church hear, and was accordingly received. He made a large confession of his faith, and an acknowledgemente of his former disorderly walking, and his being intangled with many corruptions,

W. C. Ford *et al.*, eds. (2 vols.; Boston, 1912), I, 98, 371, 402.
51. Robinson, *Works*, II, 147–48, 235, 418–23, 445.

which had been a burthen to his conscience, and blessed God for this opportunitie of freedom and libertie to injoye the ordinances of God in puritie among his people, with many more shuch like expressions." [52] Whether Lyford's confession was the product of his own volubility or of the elder's probing inquiries Bradford does not say, but Bradford was clearly impressed with the large-scale accounting which the church had received from Lyford. Bradford does not suggest, however, that the account made him or anyone else think that Lyford was one of the elect to whom God had given saving grace. Moreover, it soon became apparent that Lyford did not meet the standards of behavior required of church members. Almost at once he quarreled with the other members and started a party or "faction" against the church, actions for which he was ultimately expelled. [53]

After Lyford's departure in disgrace, Bradford says that a number of his partisans, "who before stood something of[f] from the church, now seeing Lyfords unrighteous dealing, and malignitie against the church, now tendered them selves to the church, and were joyned to the same; professing that it was not out of the dislike of any thing that they had stood of[f] so long, but a desire to fitte them selves better for shuch a state, and they saw now the Lord cald for their help." [54] Bradford does not suggest that these latecomers so suddenly fitted themselves for membership by acquiring saving grace, nor does he mention any test at all of their fitness for admission either in knowledge or behavior. He seems rather to suggest that they were received by virtue of their mere willingness to submit themselves to the church. The most recent investi-

---

52. *Plymouth Plantation*, I, 381.
53. *Ibid.*, pp. 380–419.
54. *Ibid.*, p. 406.

gation of the history of Plymouth colony likewise suggests that the churches of the colony seldom denied membership to any applicant of good behavior.[55]

Nevertheless, by 1648, we have the testimony of Governor Bradford that admission procedures in New England were stricter than they had been in Holland. In 1648 Bradford wrote "A Dialogue or the sume of a Conference between som younge men borne in New England and sundery Ancient men that came out of holland and old England." In the course of the dialogue he has the young men inquire concerning the Separatist churches of Holland: "Wherin doe they differ from the Judgment or practice of our churches heer in New England?" And the ancient men reply: "Truly for matter of practice Nothing att all that is in any thinge materiall these being Rather more strict and Ridged in some proceedings about admission of Members and things of such Nature then the other." [56] Bradford was trying to minimize the differences; and perhaps for that reason he did not go on to explain what kind of strictness or rigidity distinguished the New England churches. He may have meant simply that they examined each candidate more strictly about his understanding of Christian doctrine than had been the case in Holland. It seems probable, however, that he was referring to an additional requirement for membership, a requirement that was not part of the Separatists' practices in Holland. This requirement was clearly stated in a description of the admission procedures which the Plymouth church was following in 1669. The description was written in 1679 by John Cotton (son of the first John Cotton) who was then the minister. "The practice," he says, "was

---

55. George Langdon, "New Plymouth: A History of the Old Colony." Ph.D. dissertation, 1961, Yale University.

56. Colonial Society of Massachusetts, *Publications,* XXII (1920), 116.

for men orally to make confession of faith *and a declaration of their experiences of a worke of grace* in the prescence of the whole congregation, having bin examined and heard before by the Elders in private and then stood propounded in publick for 2 or 3 weeks ordinarily." The procedure for women differed in that their testimony was taken in private in writing and then read publicly by the pastor.[57]

Here, for the first time in our examination of admission practices, applicants for membership are required to make a declaration of their experience of a work of grace, that is, they must describe how they became convinced that they had received saving faith, and then must stand cross-examination about the experience. A test has been devised to make the church a company of people, each of whom, in his own opinion and in the opinion of the church was destined for salvation.

How did this development come about? Since Henry Ainsworth was the Separatists' ablest spokesman, it would be reasonable to suppose that the Separatists at Plymouth evolved a new admission procedure to bring their practices in line with his conception of a church. But this does not seem to have been the case. There is evidence that the admission practices which institutionalized Henry Ainsworth's view of the church were actually first established by men who were not Separatists and that from them the practice spread to the Plymouth church. It is of course possible that the Plymouth church would eventually have adopted such admission procedures even if it had been the only church in New England. But after its first decade of isolation, the Plymouth church had suddenly been surrounded by a host of Puritan immigrants from England

57. *Ibid.*, p. 145. Italics mine.

who set up new colonies and new churches. By 1640 eighteen new churches had been founded in the Massachusetts Bay colony, two in New Haven colony, three in Connecticut colony, and six in Plymouth colony. Although formal records are few, even for these churches, the movement was on so large a scale, attracted such wide attention, and caused such heated controversy that many descriptions, defenses, and attacks have survived. From these one may discern that sometime during the 1630's the new churches of New England, by introducing tests of saving faith, carried the restriction of church membership to its fullest articulation and development.

- 3 -

The New England System

꧁꧂

THE PURITANS who founded the colony of Massachusetts Bay and swarmed out into New Haven and Connecticut were not Separatists. John Winthrop, leading the first great wave of settlers in the spring of 1630, published in England, before his departure, a declaration of the colonists' attachment and gratitude to the Church of England. But once arrived in the New World, Winthrop and his companions did not scruple to construct churches closely resembling the Separatist one at Plymouth. The new churches each rested on a covenant to which all members subscribed; each chose and ordained its own ministers, admitted properly qualified new members, and expelled incorrigible old ones.[1]

The men who settled Massachusetts Bay belonged to that group of Puritans who were described in the first chapter: they believed like the Separatists in a congregational organization of the church, but unlike the Separatists they considered the churches of England, while corrupt, to be still true churches. They therefore declined to separate from them and condemned the Separatists for

1. On the nonseparating character of New England Puritanism, see Miller, *Orthodoxy in Massachusetts;* on discipline in the New England churches, see Emil Oberholzer, *Delinquent Saints* (New York, 1956).
2. John Cotton, *The Way of the Congregational Churches Cleared,*

doing so. As they themselves maintained, their intellectual pedigree ran not to Separatist divines like Robert Browne or Henry Barrow, nor even to Henry Ainsworth or John Robinson, but to the majority group of Puritans, the old Nonconformists, and particularly to William Ames, Paul Baynes, William Bradshaw, Arthur Hildersam, and Robert Parker, English divines who had acknowledged the churches of England to be true churches, even while they sought to reform them.[2]

While the pedigree is a sound one, recent historians have erred in two assumptions, first, that Ames and his colleagues had fully developed the conception of the church and of church membership later prevailing in Massachusetts, and second, that this conception was identical with the one followed by the Separatists in Holland and by the Pilgrims in Plymouth during the 1620's. Historians have assumed that the Separatists in Holland, England, and Plymouth, the nonseparating English divines, and the Puritans in Massachusetts all believed from the beginning that church membership should be limited to those who could demonstrate by a narrative of their religious experiences that they had received saving faith. The evidence adduced in the last chapter shows that in all probability no such test was applied by the Separatist churches in Holland or by the Plymouth church in the 1620's. It remains, then, to be seen where, when, and how the belief and the practice did originate of testing prospective members of the church for signs of saving grace, and thus attempting to make the visible church a spiritual approximation of the invisible church.

My contention is that the practice came, not from Plym-

pp. 13, 20; *An Apologie of the Churches in New England* (London, 1643), pp. 41–44, appended to Richard Mather, *Church Government and Church Covenant Discussed* (London, 1643); Jonathan Mitchel, *A Defence of the Answer and Arguments of the Synod* (Cambridge, Mass., 1664), pp. 4–5.

outh to Massachusetts as initially supposed, nor from England or Holland as presently assumed, but that it originated in Massachusetts among the nonseparating Puritans there and spread from Massachusetts to Plymouth, Connecticut, New Haven, and back to England. Massachusetts did not imitate Plymouth in this matter; rather the probability is that Plymouth imitated Massachusetts.

It is impossible to speak with complete certitude where much of the evidence is negative, but in order to understand the probabilities, it is necessary to begin with a consideration of the attention given by English Puritans, before the settlement of New England, to the problem of attaining and recognizing saving faith. By the time Massachusetts was founded, two generations of Puritan writers had devoted themselves to describing the processes through which God's free grace operates in the salvation of men. They had not addressed themselves to this question with a view to establishing tests for church membership. In their writings on the subject they were concerned with the individual rather than the church. They wished to trace the natural history of conversion in order to help men discover their prospects of salvation; and the result of their studies was to establish a morphology of conversion, in which each stage could be distinguished from the next, so that a man could check his eternal condition by a set of temporal and recognizable signs.[3]

Separatists did not contribute heavily to this development, partly perhaps because they were so few in number (though in Barrow, Ainsworth, and Robinson they could boast a wealth of talent) and partly because their intellectual resources were occupied in explaining and defend-

3. See for example, William Perkins, *Workes* (3 vols.; London, 1608–1631), I, 353–420, 635–44, and II, 13; Ezekiel Culverwell, *A Treatise of Faith* (London, 1623); Arthur Hildersam, *Lectures upon the*

ing their separation. It was the other Puritans, remaining within the Church of England, who mapped the route from sin to holiness and explained the way God carried a saint along it. Only through their explanation can the practices of the New England churches be understood.

The Puritans, like all Protestants, especially of the Calvinist variety, believed in predestination; God, they maintained, had determined in advance who was to be saved and who was to be damned. A man's fate was therefore decided before he entered the world of time, and his progress in this world either toward salvation or toward damnation was simply the unfolding of a decree made before he was born. Calvin had emphasized that it was impossible in this world to form a reliable opinion about whether or not a man is one of God's elect, one of those destined for salvation.[4] He had nevertheless furnished a number of clues by which anxious Christians could predict their chances. He had made it clear, for one thing, that justification (the imputation of Christ's righteousness to man) depended on faith, not works, and that sanctification (the gradual improvement of a man's behavior in obedience to God) was the product of justification rather than the cause of it. Sanctification, therefore, though it could not in itself assist a man toward salvation, could be a sign that he was saved.

Sanctification, the leading of a holy life, was not, however, a strong enough sign to offer much comfort to poor, doubting Christians, for hypocrites could do good works and so could honest but unregenerate men simply by their own volition. The real problem was to find out whether or not one had saving faith, and Puritan ministers, there-

Fourth of John (London, 1629), p. 312; William Ames, *Conscience with the Power and Cases thereof* (London, 1643), book II, in *Workes* (London, 1643).

4. Calvin, *Institutes*, II, 224.

fore, set themselves to guiding their listeners and readers in detecting faith. In a host of sermons and tracts that went far beyond Calvin, they broke down the operation of faith into a succession of recognizable stages. William Perkins, for example, whose sermons and lectures at Cambridge University brought many Englishmen to Puritanism, identified ten stages in an individual's acquisition of faith.[5] The first four were preparatory and began with attendance on the ministry of the word, which might be accompanied by some outward misfortune "to breake and subdue the stubbornness of our nature." When a man was thus made sufficiently pliable to the will of God, God brought him to a knowledge of the law, that is, a general understanding of what is good and what is evil. This understanding would eventually lead to an awareness of "his own peculiar and proper sins," which in turn led to the fourth stage, which Perkins called a "legall feare," but which later Puritans often designated as "conviction" of sin or simply as "humiliation." In this crucial stage the individual perceived his helpless and hopeless condition and despaired of salvation.[6]

Up to this point there was not necessarily any operation of saving grace; a man not destined for salvation could go this far and never get any farther. But God's elect, having arrived at a legal fear, found in their minds "a serious consideration of the promise of salvation, propounded and published in the Gospell." God then kindled a spark of faith in their hearts, that is "a will and desire to believe." But no sooner was faith kindled than a combat began in which the soul must fight against doubt and despair by

5. *Workes*, II, 13.
6. Since this stage of the process was so critical, it received a great deal of attention from Puritan writers and was often broken down into several stages. John Preston, one of the most popular of English Puritan preachers, particularly emphasized the importance of humili-

"fervent, constant, and earnest invocation for pardon."
This combat never ceased, but it eventually produced a
feeling of "assurance" and persuasion of mercy. Thereafter followed an "Evangelicall sorrow," that is, "a grief
for sin, because it is sin," and lastly God gave a man
"grace to endeavour to obey his Commandments by a
new obedience."

While all these phenomena, after the preparatory stages,
were the work of saving grace, unattainable by human
volition, they all operated through the will of the individual concerned and required his active participation. God
had made a covenant of grace with him, and by grace he
was enabled to strive against doubt and despair, to cry for
pardon and sorrow for sin. As long as he remained in the
flesh, the combat that began with the entrance of faith
would go on. Even after he reached the stage of assurance,
his doubts would continue. If they ceased, that would be
a sign that he had never had faith to begin with, but had
merely deluded himself and had not really entered into
the covenant of grace.[7]

Delusion continually threatened, because the assurance
wrought by grace was easily confused with the false assurance or "security" of the unregenerate. Arthur Hildersam explained how to distinguish true from false assurance. True assurance came only after attendance on the
preaching of the word, and only after a period of doubt
and despair. The faithful could always remember a time
"when they had the spirit of bondage in themselves, which
wrought much feare," while those with false assurance
"were never troubled with any feares or doubts this way."

ation. See *The Saints Qualification* (London, 1633), pp. 6, 31; *A Liveles
Life* (London, 1635), pp. 54–56.

7. Nonseparating Puritans developed the idea of the covenant of
grace in many of the same treatises in which they discussed the stages
of conversion. On the role of the covenant in Puritan thought, see the
writings by Perry Miller cited in Chapter 2, note 43.

The assurance of the faithful was never grounded on "a generall perswasion of Gods goodnesse, and Christs merits" or "upon some civill vertues that they discerne in themselves, which many other doe want." It rested rather on "the Testimonie of Gods Spirit." [8]

True assurance was also accompanied by the change in behavior, the obedience to God's commands that Perkins had cited as the last stage of the working of grace, and which Puritans usually called sanctification. But sanctification, though an evidence of justification, was the kind of evidence most easily mistaken. Perhaps the surest mark distinguishing true assurance from false was its continuing imperfection: "the faithfull have not this assurance so perfect, but they are oft troubled with doubts and feares. . . . But they that have this false assurance are most confident, and never have any doubts." [9]

This was the constant message of Puritan preachers: in order to be sure one must be unsure. Ezekiel Culverwell proclaimed that "an unfeigned griefe for the want of faith" [10] was a sign of faith, and William Perkins went so far as to say that "To see and feele in our selves the want of any grace pertaining to salvation, and to be grieved therefore, is the grace it selfe." [11] Though God's decrees were immutable and no man whom He had predestined to salvation could fail to attain it, the surest earthly sign of a saint was his uncertainty; and the surest sign of a damned soul was security.

Since saving faith was thus distinguished by doubt and subjected to continual combat with despair, the Puritan

8. Hildersam, *Lectures upon the Fourth of John*, p. 312.
9. *Ibid.*
10. *The Way to a Blessed Estate in This Life* (London, 1622), appended with separate pagination to *A Treatise of Faith*, p. 16.
11. *Workes*, I, 641.

was obliged to look sharp to recognize it.[12] He assisted himself by constant self-examination, frequently in writing. Puritans were prolific writers of diaries, and most of these were devoted to a daily examination of the author's assurance, which could only be bolstered by the very doubts he was seeking to overcome. It is impossible to say whether the pattern of Puritan spiritual experience was produced by the prescriptions of men like Perkins and Hildersam, or whether the prescription was itself based on experience. In any case, the operation of faith, as recorded in diaries and journals, did follow the prescription.

John Winthrop is a good example. He first felt the power of the word about the age of eighteen (1606) when he was married and went to live with his bride's family in Essex. There he attended the preaching of Ezekiel Culverwell, a nonseparating Puritan divine who wrote one of the treatises describing the operation of faith. After listening to Culverwell, Winthrop thought he could discern a change in his life. He gained a local reputation for piety, took to advising other people about their souls, and thought of entering the ministry. But he had actually not yet attained even to the stage of legal fear or conviction. Reading in Perkins [13] and other Puritan writers, he discovered that a reprobate could do as much as he had, "and now to hear others applaud mee, was a dart through my liver." But he still had not reached conviction. Instead of feeling the helplessness of his position, he redoubled his efforts to do good, and "was brought to such bondage, as I durst not use any recreation, nor meddle with any

12. "One especiall marke of a sound heart I have observed . . . is a godly jealousie of being deceived with false faith, joy and love, which maketh them carefull to examine themselves and willing to be tried by others." Culverwell, *A Treatise of Faith*, p. 57.

13. Probably *A Treatise tending unto a Declaration whether a man be in the estate of damnation, or in the estate of grace*, in *Workes*, I, 353-420.

worldly businesse, etc., for fear of breaking my peace." [14]

Finally, at about the age of thirty (1618) God brought him to a true humiliation in which "hee laid mee lower in myne owne eyes than at any time before, and shewed mee the emptines of all my guifts and parts, left mee neither power nor will, so as I became as a weaned child." With this, the work of preparation was finally ended, and "the good spirit of the Lord breathed upon my soule, and said I should live." There followed the expected trials and temptations, but the spirit never wholly deserted him: "many falls I have had, and have lyen long under some, yet never quite forsaken of the Lord." [15]

The stages are not all as clearly distinguished here as in Perkins, but the outlines of the pattern are plain: knowledge, conviction, faith, combat, and true, imperfect assurance. The pattern was repeated in hundreds of others. The marks of faith in a Puritan were painful to behold and sometimes deceptive, but they ran so much according to form, and ministers became so accustomed to advising men about them, that Calvin's injunction against seeking to discover a particular man's eternal condition seemed to be overstated. True, only God ultimately knew men's hearts, but it seemed not impossible to discern from a man's account of himself, whether his assurance was true

14. *Winthrop Papers* (Boston, 1929–   ), III, 338–44.
15. *Ibid.*
16. The earliest evidence I have found of such an inquiry in an English congregation was in Sidrach Simpson's admission to the church in Rotterdam in 1637 (Nuttall, *Visible Saints*, p. 111). But an equivocal piece of evidence from an earlier date is contained in *A Necessity of Separation from the Church of England*, ed. Charles Stovel (London, 1849), first published in 1634 by John Canne, a Separatist. According to Canne, the nonseparating Puritans maintained that candidates for membership ought "to be well informed and instructed by the elders" and ought before the church "to make a profession of faith, and to be asked sundry needful questions" (p. 186). Canne supported his statement (which was designed to show that the non-

or false, whether he had passed through conviction to faith or had merely rested in a "legal" knowledge of good and evil. If then, faith could be recognized, not with absolute certainty, but with a high degree of probability, why should not a man seeking admission to the company of the faithful demonstrate his worthiness not merely by a formal profession, by covenant, by good behavior, but also by showing that he had received true saving faith according to the established pattern by which faith had been shown to come?

Who first asked this question and answered it affirmatively is now impossible to say. By the end of the first decade of the seventeenth century, Henry Ainsworth could have done so, for he had apparently come to believe that a church should be a company of those who had saving faith. But if he did adopt a practice of inquiring into the religious experiences of prospective members, it caused no comment and no dispute in print. While the voluminous Separatist and anti-Separatist writings make clear that new members had to offer a profession, subscribe the covenant, and demonstrate good behavior, there is no mention in the period before the founding of Massachusetts, of any inquiry into the candidate's religious experiences.[16] This absence of evidence is not conclusive,

Separatists held views of membership identical with the Separatists) by marginal references to "Curt. Chu. Pow. p. 54" and "Fall of Babel, p. 30." It may be asked whether the "sundry needful questions" mentioned by Canne may not have concerned the candidate's religious experiences. The only sixteenth or seventeenth-century tract entitled *The Fall of Babel* that I have been able to discover is by John Panke (Oxford, 1608) and is evidently not the one referred to. "Curt. Chu. Pow." is James Henric, *The Curtaine of Church-power and Authoritie* (1632) and the passage in Canne appears to be based on this. On page 54, Henric describes admission procedures in French and other reformed churches as an appropriate model for England and gives the questions put to candidates in these foreign churches. All the questions concern the candidate's belief in and assent to propositions and doc-

but since so many Separatist practices were attacked and defended at length, it seems unlikely that this one would have escaped mention if it existed.

On the other hand, there is good reason for supposing the practice to have arisen among nonseparating Puritans, not only because they were so well versed in the morphology of conversion, but also because they had insisted from the beginning that faith was the indispensable criterion of a church. This was the ground on which they had refused to separate. Thomas Cartwright, who had attacked the Anglican church bitterly in the 1570's and 1580's, nevertheless refused to leave it, because the preaching of the word and administration of the sacraments brought saving faith to some of its members. With this argument he even defended the church against the attacks of the Separatists.[17] Similarly William Ames, whose theological treatises (written in the early decades of the seventeenth century) were to reign supreme in New England for a century and a half, maintained that "the profession of the true faith is the most essential note of the Church" and that "that same thing in profession doth make a Church visible, which by its inward and reall nature doth make a mysticall Church, that is, Faith." [18]

It was perhaps inevitable that Puritans who stayed within the Church of England should emphasize this invisible attribute as against the visible ones over which they had no present control. If they had conceded to the Separatists that discipline, the supervision of the members' be-

trines: "First whether he hold the doctrine taught in the old and new Testament to be Gods and sufficient to salvation? 2ly whether he hold that the reformed Churches teach and hold the same doctrine in theire Religion, and he desire to bee of it? 3 whether he hold the Pope to bee Antichrist, and the Church of Rome the whore of Babylon? And so he consenting to all this is received with joy; and there is no danger, that he should be false, or popish, who makes this profession, whereas in England, where all are admitted without any such profession they may be true, or false, as they list."

havior, was a necessary attribute of a church, then they could scarcely have defended their remaining in the English churches, which admittedly lacked the power of discipline. By stressing the importance of faith, even though they could not pretend that all or even most members of the Anglican church had it, they could claim a greater devotion to faith than the Separatists. And however specious the claim may have been, it was sufficiently dispiriting to their opponents so that Henry Ainsworth was induced to interpret the existing Separatist admission practices as tests of faith.

But the verbal duels in which the non-Separatists engaged the Separatists about the importance of faith in the church affected their own thinking as well as Henry Ainsworth's. While Ainsworth and John Robinson were groping toward a conception of the church as a company of those who possessed saving faith, non-Separatist theologians were simultaneously coming to the conclusion that saving faith not only could but should be tested. They did not develop the idea in connection with church membership, as the Separatists were doing, for in the Anglican church they were saddled with an indiscriminate membership about which they could do nothing. They developed their ideas in connection with communion, which even in the Anglican church could, in theory at least, be restricted. The Anglican Book of Common Prayer enjoined the minister to suspend "an open and notorious evil liver" from communion until he repented,[19] and non-separating Puritan ministers could use this suspending power to exclude bad actors from the Lord's Supper. But

17. Browne, *An answere to Cartwright*, pp. 86–96.
18. *The Marrow of Sacred Divinity*, in *Workes* (London, 1643), pp. 140–43.
19. *Liturgical Services: Liturgies and Occasional Forms of Prayer Set Forth in the Reign of Queen Elizabeth*, ed. W. K. Clay (Cambridge, England, 1847), p. 180.

Puritan ministers had a broader restriction in mind than the Book of Common Prayer envisaged. In their treatises they stressed the fact that only persons with saving faith were fit to take communion.[20]

I know of no instance in which a Puritan minister, before the founding of New England, actually did attempt to test the faith of communicants. Instead, Puritans stressed the individual's duty to make this examination by himself, saying that "it is not possible, that another man should by triall finde out, what is in our hearts and consciences." [21] In books and sermons on preparing for communion, they urged communicants to test themselves for the signs of faith which Perkins and the other Puritan divines had detailed for them. Indeed, this self-searching became itself a mark of faith, for "It is a signe hee sets no price upon Gods graces, that makes no inquiry whether he hath them in his possession or no. . . . For wee have no grounded hope to receive any new grace, or blessing from any ordinance of God, untill by diligent search of our selves, we have first found some former grace in our selves, that may make us (in some degree) fit and worthy receivers thereof." [22] And of course the rule held that certainty was a sign of uncertainty. A man with saving faith, who examined himself properly would find abundant evidence of his unworthiness, "So that hee doth most worthily eate and drinke this Sacrament, that shall discerne in himselfe most matter of iudgement and condemnation: and none more unworthie receivers thereof, then those which can finde nothing in themselves to iudge and condemne themselves for." [23] Although Puritan writers

20. William Bradshaw, *A Preparation to the Receiving of the Sacrament* (London, 1619), pp. 57–58; Arthur Hildersam, *The Doctrine of Communicating worthily in the Lords Supper* (London, 1619), pp. 85–92 (bound with the preceding); John Preston, *Three Sermons on the Sacrament of the Lords Supper* (London, 1631), pp. 292 ff.; *A Treatise*

stressed the individual's duty to make this examination by himself, they did not exclude the possibility of a more formal trial "which others (as farre as they are able) are to make of us, especially our Governours, Teachers, and Instructors." [24] Thus the nonseparating Puritans had at least begun to associate their highly developed morphology of conversion with an ecclesiastical institution.

There was, however, no suggestion in Puritan writings on preparation for communion that persons unfit for the Lord's Supper should also be considered unfit for church membership. And elsewhere nonseparating Congregational Puritan writers made clear that they thought of the church as including many who had given no evidence of saving faith. William Ames, for example, who emphasized faith as a mark of the church, defined a church as a society of believers, bound together by covenant; but by "believer" he did not mean one who had received saving faith, for he explicitly stated that "those who are onely believers by profession, so long as they remaine in that society are members of that Church, as also of the catholick church as touching the outward state, not touching the inward or essential state." [25]

By their refusal to separate from the Church of England, the nonseparating Puritans deprived themselves of the opportunity to put their ideas fully into practice. But some of them did attempt to achieve on a local scale and in a limited manner some of the reforms they advocated. There is evidence that a few ministers gathered together special groups from within a church or from several churches.[26]

of Effectuall Faith (London, 1631), p. 94.

21. Bradshaw, *A Preparation*, p. 76.   22. *Ibid.*, pp. 57–58.

23. *Ibid.*, p. 92.   24. *Ibid.*, p. 77.

25. *The Marrow of Sacred Divinity*, p. 140.

26. See note 34, chapter I.

The members bound themselves to one another by covenant but also remained as members of their regular parish churches. It may be that some ministers confined the communion service in their churches to such a group; but John Eliot, in recollecting his own membership in one, said that the members exercised discipline over one another but took the sacraments with other communicants in the parish church.[27] It may be also that some of these groups attempted to test the faith of prospective members, but if so no evidence of it has survived.

Only one group of non-Separatists in England is known to have actually set up an independent church. Henry Jacob (from whose name the nonseparating Congregationalists were sometimes called Jacobites) did gather a church of his own in London in 1616, as was noted earlier. It is not apparent how Jacob justified this action, for he claimed to believe that the English churches were true churches. He had disputed, corresponded, and talked with John Robinson, the pastor of the Separatist church in Leyden; and it may be that the two men reached some middle ground. Robinson certainly altered his views to accord a degree of recognition to the English churches as churches, and Jacob may have decided that gathered Congregational churches might exist side by side with the corrupt but not hopeless parish churches.[28] Jacob's church was formed by ten men, each of whom "made some confession or Profession of their Faith and Repentance, some ware longer some ware briefer, Then they Covenanted togeather to walk in all Gods Ways as he had revealed or should make known to them." [29] Subsequent members

27. *Correspondence of Baxter and Eliot*, pp. 24–25.

28. A petition by Jacob for toleration of gathered churches, dated in 1605, suggests that this may have been his view. Burrage, *Early English Dissenters*, II, 163–64. On Jacob's relations with Robinson, see *op. cit.*, I, ch. xi.

doubtless had to go through a similar procedure before admission.[30]

Without further evidence it is impossible to say whether Jacob applied any tests of faith either for admission to the church or for participation in communion. It is perhaps relevant, however, that in 1610 he argued against the view that "true Faith (acknowledged to be found in many in England) is the very Forme and essence of the Church." On the contrary, Jacob had said, "That is not so. The profession of saving faith is not the true and proper Forme of Christs Visible Church. It is the forme of each true Christian apart, and of the Church Invisible Militant and Universall." [31]

Apart from Jacob's London church, the only churches before 1630 in which nonseparating Puritans could practice with relative freedom, were in Holland. Here, in addition to the Separatist refugees, there were substantial numbers of resident English merchants and of soldiers stationed to help the Dutch against the Spaniards. These Englishmen maintained churches at Leyden, Amsterdam, and Rotterdam, presided over by nonseparating Puritans.[32] The minister of the Amsterdam, non-Separatist church, John Paget, was a bitter enemy of the Separatists and not at all friendly to people like Henry Jacob, who accepted the Separatist principles of restricting membership and of resting the church on an explicit covenant. Many of Paget's congregation, on the other hand, leaned toward these principles, and in the peculiar situation of the church in the Netherlands, the congregation had the power to elect the minister. In 1630 they attempted to choose as

29. *Op. cit.*, II, 294.
30. *Op. cit.*, I, 296, 300.
31. Jacob, *Divine Beginning*, Preface.
32. See again Stearns, *Congregationalism in the Dutch Netherlands*, Plooij, *Pilgrim Fathers from a Dutch Point of View*.

assistant to Paget the Reverend Thomas Hooker, who apparently believed, in some measure at least, in the Separatist practice of examining candidates for membership before admitting them to the church. Paget defeated the move by making Hooker answer a set of questions designed to show up his restrictive tendencies and thus alert the anti-Separatists in the congregation against him. Paget's tenth question was "Whether it be lawfull to receave any as Members into the church without publique examination of them before the whole Congregation?" Hooker answered that "some members may be receaved without publique examination, and yet the case may so fall out that some cannot without publique examination." [33]

Whether the examination Hooker envisaged was of behavior, understanding, or faith there is not a hint. This brief and inconclusive passage and the fragmentary documents of Henry Jacob's church are the only evidence extant of the procedures that non-Separatist Puritans might have adopted in the admission of members if they had had a free hand in running the churches of England.

If we turn now to New England itself, we find a mass of nonseparating Puritans pouring into the Massachusetts Bay area throughout the decade of the 1630's. The vanguard, led by John Endecott, reached Salem in 1628, and the first installment of the Great Migration, a thousand strong, arrived under John Winthrop in the summer of 1630. These men were furnished with a battery of ideas

33. Stearns, *Congregationalism in the Dutch Netherlands*, pp. 27–30, 108. The controversy also involved the question of congregational independence.

34. See Bradford's Letter Book, Massachusetts Historical Society, *Collections*, first series, (1794), III, 74–76; Walker, *Creeds and Platforms*, pp. 93–131; Miller, *Orthodoxy in Massachusetts*, pp. 102–47.

about conversion and about the church but with little or no experience in the application of those ideas. In nearby Plymouth lived a group of Separatists with very similar, though not quite identical ideas, and with many years' experience. When the non-Separatists prepared to found their first congregationally organized churches, it would not have been surprising if they had consulted the more experienced brethren at Plymouth, and all the evidence indicates that they did so. In the spring of 1629 Deacon Samuel Fuller of Plymouth visited Salem, and John Endecott discovered that Fuller's view of the church closely resembled his own. A few weeks later the Salem church was founded. During the summer of 1630 when the next churches were being formed, Fuller again visited the Bay area, accompanied this time by Edward Winslow, one of Plymouth's acknowledged leaders. The two conferred with the Massachusetts people about church matters.[34] Early historians of Puritanism, assuming that only Separatists believed in congregationally organized churches and that all other Puritans were Presbyterians, thought that the Plymouth men converted the Salem men to Congregationalism and that the Salem men converted the subsequent Massachusetts settlers.[35] Champlin Burrage, Perry Miller, and Raymond Stearns have now demonstrated the existence of a nonseparating group of Puritans who were disposed toward Congregationalism, and who founded and settled the colony of Massachusetts Bay.[36] Such Puritans needed no transformation before they were ready to

35. An exception was Joseph Fletcher, *The History of the Revival and Progress of Independency in England* (4 vols.; London, 1847–1849), III, 125–30, whose account of the Massachusetts Puritans anticipated much modern scholarship. For this reference I am indebted to an unpublished paper by Caroline Lowe Brown.

36. Burrage, *Early English Dissenters*, I, 281–368; Miller, *Orthodoxy in Massachusetts*; Stearns, *Congregationalism in the Dutch Netherlands*.

gather independent churches of limited membership. But since Congregationalism was not yet a fully worked out system in England or even a distinct movement, there was still room for Massachusetts to learn from Plymouth.[37]

Fuller and Winslow and possibly other Plymouth people must have given a good deal of needed advice about procedures, and in the first years of the Bay colony the Massachusetts churches probably learned much from the Pilgrims, including some practices they later abandoned, such as "prophesying" by laymen and the question and answer period after the sermon.[38] What they did not learn was to apply tests of saving faith to candidates for membership. The surviving contemporary references to the founding of the Salem church say nothing of such a procedure, nor do later seventeenth century accounts. Since the Salem church has generally been regarded by historians as the prototype of Massachusetts Bay churches, it may be worth examining these accounts in some detail.

The first full description of the founding of the Salem church was published in 1669 by Nathaniel Morton, then secretary of Plymouth Colony. Morton had come to Plymouth in 1623 at the age of eleven. There is no evidence that he was present at the founding of the Salem church, and he wrote his account many years after the event as part of a history of New England. But while most of his history of the early years is simply a paraphrase or transcription of Bradford's manuscript, he offered a good deal

37. Larzer Zif, "The Salem Puritans in the 'Free Aire of a New World,'" *Huntington Library Quarterly*, XX (1957), 373–84, has attemped to restore the old view that Salem was converted by Plymouth. His principal evidence is Baillie's citation of Cotton's letter to Skelton, but he apparently did not have access to the text of the letter (see below, note 41). Although in my opinion he has exaggerated the change effected in the Salem group, the text of the letter supports his argument for a Separatist influence at Salem. The point I wish to stress is not that there was an alteration in the Salem group from Presbyterianism to Congregationalism — for I believe this was not the case —

more detail about Salem than Bradford had done. He tells us that Francis Higginson and Samuel Skelton, both of whom had been "Non-conformists" in England, coming to Salem in June, 1629, agreed with Governor John Endecott and the other godly inhabitants to found "a Reformed Congregation." Accordingly, his account proceeds:

> they pitched upon the 6th of *August* for their entring into a solemn Covenant with God, and one another, and also for the Ordaining of their Ministers; of which they gave notice to the Church of *Plimouth* (that being the onely Church that was in the Country before them) the people made choice of Mr. *Skelton* for their Pastor, and Mr. *Higginson* for their Teacher. And accordingly it was desired of Mr. *Higginson* to draw up a Confession of Faith and Covenant in Scripture-language; which being done, was agreed upon. . . . Thirty Copies of the foresaid *Confession of Faith* and *Covenant* being written out for the use of thirty persons who were to begin the Work. When the sixth of *August* came, it was kept as a day of Fasting and Prayer, in which after the Sermons and Prayers of the two Ministers, in the end of the day, the foresaid *Confession of Faith* and *Covenant* being solemnly read, the forenamed persons did solemnly profess their Consent thereunto: and then proceeded to the Ordaining of Mr. *Skelton* Pastor, and Mr. *Higginson* Teacher of the Church there. Mr. *Bradford* the Governour of *Plimouth*, and some others with him, coming by Sea, were hindred by cross winds that they could not be there at the beginning of the day, but they came into the Assembly afterward, and gave

but rather that the settlers of Massachusets Bay had not previously worked out the details of Congregational polity. Geoffrey Nuttall has maintained that Congregationalism in England was not fully developed before the 1640's (*Visible Saints*, pp. 8–14); and the reason is obvious: few Englishmen in England had had experience before the 1640's in forming or running a Congregational church.

38. Winthrop records a number of instances of prophesying in the early churches of Massachusetts. See *The History of New England,* ed. James Savage (2 vols.; Boston, 1853), I, 109, 144. Cf. Baillie, *Dissuasive,* p. 174; Cotton Mather, *Magnalia Christi Americana* (London, 1702), book VII, p. 18.

them the *right hand of fellowship,* wishing all prosperity, and a blessed success unto such good beginnings. After which, at several times many others joyned to the Church in the same way. The *Confession of Faith* and *Covenant* fore-mentioned, was acknowledged onely as a Direction pointing unto that Faith and Covenant contained in the holy Scripture, and therefore no man was confined unto that form of words, but onely to the Substance, End and Scope of the matter contained therein: And for the Circumstantial manner of joyning to the Church, it was ordered according to the wisdome and faithfulness of the Elders; together with the liberty and ability of any person. Hence it was, that some were admitted by expressing their Consent to that written *Confession of Faith* and *Covenant;* others did answer to questions about the Principles of Religion that were publickly propounded to them; some did present their Confession in writing, which was read for them, and some that were able and willing, did make their Confession in their own words and way: A due respect was also had unto the Conversations of men, *viz.* that they were without Scandal.[39]

The next account of the founding occurs in a history of New England completed about 1682 by the Reverend William Hubbard, who was born in 1621 and graduated from Harvard in the class of 1642. Though not present at the founding, he was later minister at nearby Ipswich and could have talked with some of those who were present. His account is derived largely from Morton's, but he adds one detail which confirms the observation we have already made, that the Congregational system had not yet been fully worked out by the nonseparating Puritans of Massa-

39. Nathaniel Morton, *New-Englands Memoriall* (Cambridge, Mass., 1669; Boston, 1903), pp. 75–76.
40. William Hubbard, *A General History of New England from the Discovery to 1680.* Second edition, collated with the original manuscript, ed. William T. Harris (Boston, 1848), pp. 117–20, 181–82.
41. John Cotton to Samuel Skelton, Oct. 2, 1630, in Thaddeus M.

chusetts before their departure from England. Arthur Hildersam, he says, had urged the ministers who contemplated going to New England to agree in advance upon a form of church organization. No such agreement was reached before the exodus began, not apparently because of any positive disagreements, but because they had not yet thought out the details of what they wanted. "They had not," Hubbard says, "as yet, waded so far into the controversy of church discipline [i.e., the controversy between Presbyterians and Congregationalists] as to be very positive in any of those points wherein the main hinge of the controversy lay between them and others." Hubbard, like Morton, gives no hint of any test of saving faith at Salem; and the probability that there was none is reinforced by his description of the first Massachusetts churches founded after Salem's: "in the beginning of things they only accepted of one another, according to some general profession of the doctrine of the Gospel, and the honest and good intentions they had one towards another." [40]

One indirect but primary piece of evidence strengthens the impression gained from Morton and Hubbard that no experience of saving grace was necessary for membership in the Salem church. The Reverend John Cotton, who did not arrive in New England until 1633, having heard about certain proceedings at Salem in the summer of 1630 (from whom it is not clear) wrote a disapproving letter to Samuel Skelton on October 2, 1630.[41] Cotton complained that the Salem group upon the arrival of the first great wave of set-

---

Harris, *Memorials of the First Church in Dorchester* (Boston, 1830), pp. 53–57. Harris prints this letter from a transcript made by Richard Mather, June 13, 1631. It is the letter referred to in Baillie, *Dissuasive*, pp. 54–55, 65. The existence in Harris's *Memorials* of a text of this important document, which recent historians have discussed but not read, was discovered and brought to my attention by David Hall.

tlers had refused to baptize one man's child and had denied the Lord's Supper to several other worthy men, including Governor Winthrop, because they were not members of any particular reformed church (the new arrivals were not yet organized in churches of their own). Skelton had compounded this offense, according to Cotton, by admitting "one of Mr. Lathrop's congregation not only to the Lord's Supper, but his child to baptism upon sight of his testimony from his Church, whereas Mr. Coddington, bringing the same from the Chief of our Congregation, was not accepted."

Mr. Lathrop was John Lathrop,[42] and his congregation was the one founded in London in 1616 by Henry Jacob. The Salem church thus seemed to recognize a bond with this congregationally organized, though technically non-separating, church but not with the regular parish churches of England. If Cotton's information was correct, the Salem church was taking a Separatist position.[43]

The proceedings at Salem, in Cotton's view, evinced a too literal adherence, typical of Separatism, to the principle that a true church must rest on a covenant. Cotton rebuked the Salem leaders on two grounds: "*first,* that you think no man may be admitted to the Sacrament though a member of a Catholic Church, unless he be a member of some particular Reformed Church. *Secondly,* that none of the congregations in England are particular Reformed Churches but Mr. Lathrop's and such as his." Actually Cotton had himself gathered a special group in England, evidently by an implicit or tacit covenant, to take communion. Like other nonseparating Puritans he had not

42. It may be significant that when Lathrop himself came to New England in 1634, he settled not in non-Separatist Massachusetts, but in Scituate, in the Plymouth colony.

43. It is perhaps no accident that the ardently Separatist Roger Wil-

fully thought out his own views on church polity and considered the explicit church covenants of the Separatists to be desirable rather than essential. To Skelton he wrote that "an explicit Covenant is rather a solemn vow to bind the members of the Church together in nearer fellowship with God and one another, than any such essential cause of a Church without which it cannot be." Cotton charged Skelton with leaning too heavily on the Separatists at Plymouth. "You went hence," he said, "of another judgment, and I am afraid your change hath sprung from New Plymouth men, whom, though I much esteem as godly and loving Christians, yet their grounds which they have received for this tenent from Mr. Robinson, do not justify me, though the man I reverence as godly and learned." [44]

Cotton's censorious letter is one more indication that nonseparating Puritans, who inclined toward a Congregational polity, had not yet worked out the details of it as fully as the Separatists had. One detail that Cotton had obviously not thought through was that of establishing proper qualifications for receiving the sacraments. Since he thought Salem was too restrictive in its baptismal and communion practices, it seems likely that if the Salem church had required a special test of saving faith for membership, Cotton would at this time have complained of it even more strongly than he did of the church's denial of the sacraments to deserving nonmembers.

It seems probable, then, that the procedures of the first Massachusetts church in admitting members, were similar to those of the Plymouth church and of the Separatist churches in England and Holland, and that none of these

liams, upon discovering that the Boston church acknowledged the churches of England to be true, proceeded to Salem and later became minister there. Cf. Zif, "The Salem Puritans in the 'Free Aire of a New World.'"

44. Harris, *Memorials*, pp. 53–57.

tested members for an experience of saving faith. But within ten years the procedures for founding a church and admitting new members to it did include such a test. During this decade some twenty thousand settlers landed in New England, and eighteen churches were set up in Massachusetts alone. By 1640 the New Englanders had evolved practices so uniform that both critics and advocates could agree in describing them, and evidence is so abundant that we need not resort to speculation.[45]

The founding or "gathering" of a church began with at least seven men, who had to satisfy one another both about their knowledge of Christian doctrine *and* about their experience of saving grace. The ministers of some nearby churches had to be present along with some of the civil magistrates of the colony. If these experts thought the prospective founders of the church to be not properly qualified, the group was obliged to wait until suitable saints were forthcoming. Once a church was gathered, by subscription of the first members to a covenant, it elected officers: a pastor or teacher (or both in a large congregation) and a ruling elder or elders and deacons. Then, as qualified candidates appeared, it admitted new members.

Because the procedure for admission occasioned much dispute between the Puritans of New England and old, the details of it are fully recorded. A person seeking admission to the church first approached the elders who in a personal interview examined both his knowledge and his religious experiences. Any obviously ignorant, "graceless," or scandalous person was turned back then and there. But if the examination was satisfactory the ruling elder pro-

45. The ensuing account is based on the detailed descriptions offered by John Cotton, *The Way of the Churches of Christ in New England* (London, 1645), pp. 6–10, 54–58; Richard Mather, *Church Government and Church Covenant Discussed* (London, 1643), pp. 23–24;

posed the candidate to the church, requesting the members to make inquiry about him. Members were expected to report any known offense committed by the candidate and he was required to explain or show his repentance for it, in private for private offenses and before the church for public ones.

If the candidate passed these hurdles, several members testified at a church meeting to his good behavior, and he was called upon to demonstrate the work of God in his soul. For women and for men who were excessively diffident, the elders might simply repeat to the church the result of their private examination of the candidate but normally he was expected to make a narration, perhaps fifteen minutes in length, of the way in which God's saving grace came to him. Questions might be put to him about this experience by any member in order that all might be certain of its genuineness; and in some cases the whole demonstration may have consisted of questions and answers.

If the members or a majority of them were satisfied by the narration, the candidate went on to make a profession of faith, that is, a statement of the main doctrines of Christianity in which he believed. Though at first the candidate might state his beliefs in his own words, the profession or confession ultimately became standardized, but differed in wording from church to church. Following it the members voted on the candidate's admission. The ruling elder then tendered him the church covenant, which he assented to with relation to the church and the church with relation to him. With this action he became a member.

Although these procedures were probably more elab-

Thomas Lechford, *Plain Dealing*, ed. J. Hammond Trumbull (Boston, 1867), pp. 12–29; Edward Johnson, *A History of New England* (*Wonder-Working Providence*), ed. J. F. Jameson (New York, 1910), pp. 214–17. Cotton's and Mather's tracts were written some years before the publication dates.

orate than those of the Separatist churches in Holland, the only radical difference from the Separatist practice lay in the candidate's demonstration of the work of grace in his soul. Inquiry into his good behavior, the profession of faith, and the subscription to the covenant had all been practiced by the Separatists. But the demonstration of saving grace was a distinct addition. It meant that every member of a New England church must be able to describe personal experiences corresponding to those which theologians like Perkins and Hildersam had defined. According to Thomas Lechford, an unfriendly witness, the candidates had to show "that they have beene wounded in their hearts for their originall sinne, and actuall transgressions, and can pitch upon some promise of free grace in the Scripture, for the ground of their faith, and that they finde their hearts drawne to beleeve in Christ Jesus, for their justifica- tion and salvation, and these in the ministerie of the Word, reading or conference." [46] John Cotton, teacher of the Boston church, has left on record some of the questions normally put to candidates there: "How it pleased God to worke in them, to bring them home to Christ, whether the law have convinced them of sinne, how the Lord hath wonne them to deny themselves and their owne righteous- nesse, and to rely on the righteousnesse of Christ." [47]

Some narratives were written down, either by the can- didate or by the elders (the Reverend Michael Wiggles- worth took down several in shorthand in his diary).[48] A number of these have survived, and they demonstrate clearly the familiarity of the narrators with the morphol- ogy of conversion, a familiarity produced, no doubt, by

46. *Plain Dealing*, p. 19.
47. *A Coppy of a Letter of Mr. Cotton* (1641), p. 5.
48. "The Diary of Michael Wigglesworth," ed. E. S. Morgan, Co- lonial Society of Massachusetts, *Publications*, XXXV (1942–1946), 426–

a great many sermons on the subject. The pattern is so plain as to give the experiences the appearance of a stereotype: first comes a feeble and false awakening to God's commands and a pride in keeping them pretty well, but also much backsliding. Disappointments and disasters lead to other fitful hearkenings to the word. Sooner or later true legal fear or conviction enables the individual to see his hopeless and helpless condition and to know that his own righteousness cannot save him, that Christ is his only hope. Thereafter comes the infusion of saving grace, sometimes but not always so precisely felt that the believer can state exactly when and where it came to him. A struggle between faith and doubt ensues, with the candidate careful to indicate that his assurance has never been complete and that his sanctification has been much hampered by his own sinful heart.

If the candidate neglected any point, the elders or the members might question him about it. An exchange recorded by Michael Wigglesworth is typical. A candidate was asked: "Do you never find a heart that can't prize Christ but had rather walk after the way of your own heart?" If he had answered that he always prized Christ above all else, he would have failed the test. His actual answer was perfectly phrased: "Yes I have seen it many a time but I have considered that was the way to ruin both me and mine after me. I have searched to see whether I loved God's company or no and I have found indeed my opposition against it. Yet I have found in some poor measure that God hath helped me to take delight in his will." [49] This was faith in its proper imperfection, and one may be

44. Thomas Shepard recorded fifty narratives of members admitted to the Cambridge church. The manuscript is in the possession of the New England Historic Genealogical Society. I have consulted the photostat copy in the Massachusetts Historical Society.

49. *Ibid.*, p. 440.

sure that the candidate was admitted. On the other hand, Captain John Underhill was clearly on shaky ground when he sought admission to the church by asserting with full assurance that saving grace had come to him while he was enjoying a pipe of the good creature tobacco.[50]

Sometimes the candidate might entertain the church with an all too lengthy spiritual autobiography. So at least we may infer from Thomas Shepard, who felt obliged to defend this part of the admission procedure against the objection that "there are many odd confessions by those that are received, and extravagant enlarged discourses of the set time of their conversion, and their Revelation, and ill Application of Scripture which makes such long doings, and are wearisome and uncomely." To this objection Shepard answered with a prescription for a proper narrative. "I confess," he said, "it is not fit that so holy and solemn an Assembly as a Church is, should be held long with Relations of this odd thing and tother, nor hear of Revelations and groundless joyes, nor gather together the heap, and heap up all the particular passages of their lives, wherein they have got any good; nor Scriptures and Sermons, but such as may be of special use unto the people of God, such things as tend to shew, Thus I was humbled, then thus I was called, then thus I have walked, though with many weaknesses since, and such special providences of God I have seen, temptations gone through, and thus the Lord hath delivered me, blessed be his Name &c."[51]

The introduction of this new spiritual test for membership was not accompanied by any relaxation in the old demand that members demonstrate knowledge of the prin-

50. Winthrop, *History*, I, 324–25.
51. Thomas Shepard, *The Parable of the Ten Virgins* (London, 1660), II, 200. Though published in 1660, this work was based on

ciples of religion, that they voluntarily assent to the covenant, and that they live lives free of scandal. The New
England churches were fully equipped with powers of
discipline and exercised them to expel members who lapsed
from good behavior. But the new demand for signs of
grace gave the New England churches a different character from the old Separatist churches. In England and
Holland, anyone who wished to join a Separatist church
could qualify himself to do so by actions that lay within
his own power. In New England, membership required
an experience that was beyond the power of a man to attain by his own efforts. Hypocrites might dissemble it,
and the New Englanders were the first to admit that their
churches contained hypocrites; they did not dream of
perfection in this world, and they joined the chorus against
the Donatists and Anabaptists.[52] But they held it a duty to
exclude from the church everyone who failed to persuade
them in speech or writing that he possessed saving grace.
While affirming the old distinction between the visible
and the invisible church, they thus narrowed the distance
between the two far more drastically than the Separatists
had done.

It is certain that the new system was fully established
in Massachusetts by 1640; yet it is highly probable that
it did not exist in 1629. How, then, did it come into existence?

The evidence is fragmentary. Cotton Mather, writing in
1701, when the system was under attack and he and his
father were defending it, related a tradition, which he did
not attempt to refute, that:

sermons preached 1636–1640.
52. Perry Miller, *The New England Mind: From Colony to Province*
(Cambridge, Mass., 1953), pp. 68–81.

. . . the first Churches of *New England* began only with a Profession of Assent and Consent unto the *Confession of Faith* and the *Covenant* of Communion. Afterwards, they that sought for the Communion, were but privately examined about a Work of *Grace* in their Souls, by the *Elders*, and then publickly propounded unto the Congregation, only that so, if there were any scandal in their Lives, it might be objected and considered. But in the year 1634, one of the Brethren having leave to hear the Examinations of the *Elders*, magnified so much the Advantage of being present at such an Exercise, that many others desired and obtained the like leave to be present at it; until, at length, to gratifie this useful *Curiosity*, the whole Church always expected the *Liberty* of being thus particularly acquainted with the *Religious Dispositions* of those with whom they were afterwards to sit at the Table of the Lord; and that Church which *began* this way was quickly imitated by most of the rest. . . .[53]

Cotton Mather was writing long after the event, without firsthand knowledge but from a wide acquaintance with the writings, published and unpublished, of the founders. William Hubbard, who graduated from Harvard in the first class in 1642, was a little closer to the events. His account, from which I have already quoted, confirms Mather's and offers a further detail:

Those that came over soon after Mr. Endicot, namely Mr. Higginson and Mr. Skelton, Anno 1629, walked something in an untrodden path; therefore it is the less to be wondered at, if they went but in and out, in some things complying

53. *Magnalia*, book V, p. 43.
54. Hubbard, *General History*, pp. 181–82. Cf. Mather, *Magnalia*, book III, pp. 20–21: "There were divers Churches gathered in the Country, before the Arrival of Mr. *Cotton;* but upon his Arrival, the Points of *Church-Order*, were with more of Exactness revived, and received in them, and *further* observed in such as were gathered after them."
55. Hubbard, *General History*, p. 186. It would not be surprising if

too much, in some things too little, with those of the Separation, and it may be in some things not sufficiently attending to the order of the Gospel, as themselves thought they understood afterwards. For in the beginning of things they only accepted of one another, according to some general profession of the doctrine of the Gospel, and the honest and good intentions they had one towards another, and so by some kind of covenant moulded themselves into a church in every Plantation, where they took up their abode, until Mr. Cotton and Mr. Hooker came over, which was in the year 1633, who did clear up the order and method of church government, according as they apprehended was most consonant to the Word of God. And such was the authority they (especially Mr. Cotton) had in the hearts of the people, that whatever he delivered in the pulpit was soon put into an Order of Court, if of a civil, or set up as a practice in the church, if of an ecclesiastical concernment. After that time the administration of all ecclesiastical matters was tied up more strictly than before to the rules of that which is since owned for the Congregational Way. . . .[54]

Hubbard also tells us that George Phillips, the minister of Watertown who came to New England with Winthrop in 1630, "was, at the first, more acquainted with the way of church discipline, since owned by Congregational churches; but being then without any to stand by him, . . . he met with much opposition from some of the magistrates, till the time that Mr. Cotton came into the country, who, by his preaching and practice, did by degrees mould all their church administrations into the very same form which Mr. Phillips labored to have introduced into the churches before." [55]

the Watertown church was somewhat more forward than the others in Congregationalism, because at least one member of it, Richard Brown, the ruling elder, had had experience in the practice of Congregationalism before coming to the New World. Brown had been one of the founders of Henry Jacob's church in London in 1616. See Hubbard, *General History*, p. 187; Burrage, *Early English Dissenters*, II, 294.

Hubbard, then, assigns to John Cotton a key role in the establishment of the New England system as it became known to later generations. Since most of the other elements of this system were already present in the Salem church, Hubbard would seem to make Cotton the principal author of the test of saving faith, which became the distinguishing feature of the system.

Now Cotton, as we have seen, had been opposed in 1630 to some of the features of Congregationalism as adopted in Salem; and it is impossible to say exactly when his views changed. In a sermon preached at Salem in 1636 he acknowledged that they had indeed changed, not because of arguments that Skelton had sent in answer to his letter of 1630 (he lost the answer before reading it!) but because of reasons he had found in his own study of Scripture.[56] But the change probably occurred not long after the receipt of Skelton's letter, for by the time Cotton left England in 1633 he seems to have come around to the view that a church must be gathered by explicit covenant, and that a minister can offer the sacraments only to members of the congregation that have called him to office. This is indicated by a passage in John Winthrop's Journal that describes the statement of principles which Cotton made when admitted to the Boston church:

---

56. John Cotton, *A Sermon Preached by the Reverend Mr. John Cotton . . . at Salem, 1636, To which is Prefaced a Retraction of his former Opinion . . .* (Boston, 1713).

57. Winthrop, *History*, I, 131.

58. On Cotton's divergence from other New England ministers, especially Hooker, in this matter, see Perry Miller, "Preparation for Salvation in Seventeenth-Century New England," *Journal of the History of Ideas*, IV (1943), 253–86 and Cotton's *Sermon at Salem*, pp. 27–32. Additional evidence of Cotton's divergent views will be found in two documents in the British Public Record Office (C.O. 1/9, f. 159 and ff. 160–65). These documents, received in England in October, 1637, show Cotton arguing that sanctification cannot be a first evidence of

On Saturday evening, the congregation met in their ordinary exercise, and Mr. Cotton, being desired to speak to the question, (which was of the church,) he showed, out of the Canticles, 6, that some churches were as queens, some as concubines, some as damsels, and some as doves, etc. He was then (with his wife) propounded to be admitted a member. The Lord's day following, he exercised in the afternoon, and being to be admitted, he signified his desire and readiness to make his confession according to order, which he said might be sufficient in declaring his faith about baptism, (which he then desired for his child, born in their passage, and therefore named Seaborn). He gave two reasons why he did not baptize it at sea, (not for want of fresh water, for he held, sea water would have served:) 1, because they had no settled congregation there; 2, because a minister hath no power to give the seals but in his own congregation.[57]

By this account, Cotton at his arrival in Massachusetts held views of the church and ministry that he had condemned in his letter to Skelton in 1630.

Shortly after his arrival Cotton was elected teacher of the Boston church. The predominant aspect of his teaching, if we may judge by his published work, was an emphasis on the importance of faith and of unmerited saving grace. Indeed, he seems to have stressed unmerited saving grace more than any other non-Separatist minister and to have placed the coming of faith at a somewhat later stage in the morphology of conversion.[58] He also insisted that

justification, that faith is passive in justification, and that preparation for salvation cannot include any "gracious Condicions or Qualifications wrought in the Soule before Faith." Although Cotton was defeated in these views, especially the last, during the Antinomian crisis, it is perhaps significant, in the light of Hooker's departure for Connecticut in 1636, that one of the documents (f. 159) states that Hooker alone believed in "any saving preparation in a Christian soule before his unyon with Christ" and that "the rest of the Ministers do not concurr with him: Cotton and the rest of the contrary opinion are against him and his party in all." I have examined these documents in the Library of Congress microfilm.

faith was the principal ingredient of a true church and that a church covenant formed on any other basis was a covenant of works only.[59]

Soon after Cotton took office in the Boston church a religious revival occurred there. Winthrop tells us that "More were converted and added to that church, than to all the other churches in the bay," and that "Divers profane and notorious evil persons came and confessed their sins, and were comfortably received into the bosom of the church." [60] One of the members added in 1634 was Winthrop's son, and Winthrop's Journal indicates that the young man was admitted only after several months of despair about his own condition: "yet attending to the means, and not giving over prayer, and seeking counsel, etc., he came at length to be freed from his temptations, and to find comfort in God's promises, and so, being received into the congregation, upon good proof of his understanding in the things of God, he went on cheerfully in a Christian course, ..." [61] Although Winthrop does not indicate that his son offered the church a narrative of these experiences, they did follow, as Winthrop describes them, the standard pattern of conversion found in later narratives by candidates. It would appear to be significant that the young man did not join the church until after he had undergone these experiences.

In the absence of further evidence it is impossible to tell whether the Boston church at this time demanded that candidates describe their conversion, but it may be that Cotton's religious revival prompted converts, before admission to the church, voluntarily to narrate the experi-

59. Cotton, *Sermon at Salem*, p. 24.
60. Winthrop, *History*, I, 144; cf. *Chronicles of the First Planters of the Colony of Massachusetts Bay*, ed. Alexander Young (Boston, 1846), pp. 354–55.

ences that led them to the step. Perhaps Winthrop was referring to such narrations when he recorded in his Journal that certain evil persons "confessed their sins" before admission. He follows his description of their admission with the words: "Yea, the Lord gave witness to the exercise of prophecy, so as thereby some were converted, and others much edified." [62] Winthrop may thus be equating "the exercise of prophecy" with whatever relation the converts delivered to the church.

Prophecy, it will be recalled, was the practice favored by the Separatists of supplementing (or, in the absence of a minister, replacing) the sermon with speeches by members of the congregation. It is known that in one Congregational church in Ireland in 1653 narratives of conversion were used both as a test of candidates for admission and as a form of prophesying.[63] And Cotton Mather's account of the origin of the new test suggests that initially it was regarded as serving the same dual function in Massachusetts. Though prophesying was shortly abandoned in most Massachusetts churches (but not, however, abandoned in Plymouth colony), it may be that the narratives of candidates were an outgrowth of prophesying and that the Boston church is the one referred to by Cotton Mather.

Whatever the practices of the Boston church in 1634, by the next year a number of ministers, whether prompted by Cotton or by their own reasoning, had decided that evidence of a work of grace in the heart, or in other words, saving faith, was a necessary qualification for church membership. In that year the people of the church at Newtown

61. Winthrop, *History*, I, 149.
62. *Ibid.*, p. 144.
63. J. H. Taylor, "Some Seventeenth-Century Testimonies," Congregational Historical Society, *Transactions*, XVI (1949–1951), 64–77.

(later Cambridge) led by Thomas Hooker were preparing to depart for the richer lands of the Connecticut Valley. In their places a group led by Thomas Shepard was moving into Newtown, with the intention of founding a new church of their own. The newcomers asked the approbation of the magistrates and the guidance of the neighboring ministers in the proper method of doing it and were told "that such as were to join should make confession of their faith, *and declare what work of grace the Lord had wrought in them.*" [64]

The following year, 1636, a new church was proposed at Dorchester for the same reason as at Newtown: a new group was taking the place of one departing for Connecticut. Again the magistrates and a number of neighboring ministers were called on for approbation and advice, and they attended the ceremonies to offer it, Thomas Shepard among them. This time the advisers (apparently led by Thomas Shepard) halted the proceedings, because the men who proposed to found the church, after making a satisfactory confession of faith, were unable properly to "manifest the work of God's grace in themselves." Winthrop says:

The reason was for that most of them (Mr. Mather and one more excepted) had builded their comfort of salvation upon unsound grounds, viz., some upon dreams and ravishes of spirit by fits; others upon the reformation of their lives; others upon duties and performances, etc; wherein they discovered three special errors: 1. That they had not come to hate sin, because it was filthy, but only left it, because it was hurtful. 2. That, by reason of this, they had never truly closed with Christ, (or rather Christ with them,) but had

64. Winthrop, *History*, I, 215. Italics mine.
65. *Ibid.*, pp. 218–19. Cf. *Winthrop Papers*, III, 244; Thomas Shepard to Richard Mather, April 2, 1636, in J. A. Albro, *The Life of Thomas*

made use of him only to help the imperfection of their sanctification and duties, and not made him their sanctification,
wisdom, etc. 3. They expected to believe by some power of
their own, and not only and wholly from Christ.[65]

In other words, the proposed founders of the Dorchester
church were insufficiently familiar with the morphology
of conversion and so had deceived themselves.

The new test was evidently becoming entrenched.
There was more than a hint of compulsion in the quash-
ing of the proposed second church of Dorchester. The
magistrates who attended must also at that time have been
participating in the March meeting of the General Court,
and their experience at Dorchester was probably the occasion for the law which the General Court enacted at this
session:

Forasmuch as it hath bene found by sad experience, that
much trouble and disturbance hath happened both to the
church and civill state by the officers and members of some
churches, which have bene gathered within the limitts of this
jurisdiccion in a undue manner, and not with such publique
approbacion as were meete, it is therefore ordered that all
persons are to take notice that this Court doeth not, nor will
hereafter, approve of any such companyes of men as shall
henceforth joyne in any pretended way of church fellow-
shipp, without they shall first acquainte the magistrates and
the elders of the greater parte of the churches in this jurisdiccion, with their intencions, and have their approbacion
herein. And ffurther, it is ordered, that noe person, being a
member of any churche which shall hereafter be gathered
without the approbacion of the magistrates, and the greater
parte of the said churches, shalbe admitted to the ffreedome
of this commonwealthe.[66]

Shepard (Boston, 1870), pp. 212–18.
66. *Records of the Governor and Company of the Massachusetts
Bay*, ed. N. B. Shurtleff (5 vols.; Boston, 1853–1854), I, 168.

This enactment, though it did not prescribe details, may be taken as the official establishment of the new system. Although the Dorchester episode was probably the immediate occasion of the law, the colony's troubles with Roger Williams, who went to Rhode Island in January, 1636, may also have had something to do with it. Williams was an avowed Separatist and the Salem church, where he preached from 1633 to 1635, had shown at its inception certain Separatist tendencies which John Cotton had denounced. Williams tried to carry Salem into a separation not merely from the churches of England but from the other Massachusetts churches as well. As a result of strong pressure from the civil government, Williams failed, was banished, and departed for Rhode Island in 1636.

Later in that year John Cotton visited Salem and preached the sermon we have already noticed in which he admitted his change of mind about the need for explicit church covenants. In that sermon Cotton coupled his observations on church covenants with an insistence on faith as the indispensable quality of a true church. He denounced separation from any church in which faith was present, and he warned against covenants that made any other requirement necessary to a church. "Build a Church upon any other foundation but Faith, and the profession of Faith," he said, "and it will break into manifold distempers." [67] Cotton rehearsed the standard signs of faith, emphasizing the need for thorough and continuing humiliation and doubt, and minimizing the efficacy of all human efforts. "If you come to Christ by vertue of any thing which is in you," he warned, "it is but a legal work." And if the church bestowed membership on persons who had no other qualifications than their good behavior and their zeal for reformation of church practices, "they will breed

67. Cotton, *Sermon at Salem*, p. 24.

distraction in your Churches . . . look to it carefully, when they come into the Church, for otherwise you will find everlasting confusion, rather than an everlasting Covenant." [68] Cotton was indicting the Separatists for their preoccupation with behavior: church covenants which aimed only at good behavior and reformation of the forms of worship were mere covenants of works.

Having discovered the importance of explicit church covenants, Cotton, like Ainsworth, has identified them with the covenant of grace, but has gone beyond Ainsworth to give ecclesiastical, institutional expression to that identification. He has concluded that the signs of faith which the earlier non-Separatist Puritans had developed as necessary for participation in the covenant of grace were just as necessary for participation in the church covenant. "Let the Church look to her Covenant," he says, "and let no Member come in but he that *Knoweth Christ*, and that knoweth he is a *Child of Wrath;* and let him go on, not in his own Strength, but in a depending frame upon Jesus Christ, and then all the World will know that you have made an Everlasting Covenant." [69]

It is not clear whether the Salem church had by this time adopted the new test and thus made its covenant everlasting, but Cotton implied that it had not and also that it was still tainted with Separatism. If the observations about Separatist practices offered in the previous chapter are correct, and if Salem was influenced by the Plymouth Separatists, these two charges are completely compatible and highly plausible. The sequel to Cotton's visit came in December, 1636, when the Salem church installed Cotton's admirer, the Reverend Hugh Peter, as minister, and adopted a new covenant in which the members expressly

68. *Ibid.,* p. 32.   69. *Ibid.,* p. 27.

disclaimed any Separatist tendency ("noe way sleighting our sister Churches, but useing theire Counsell as need shalbe") and promised to submit "to those that are over us, in Church or Commonweale, knowing how well pleasing it will be to the Lord, that they should have incouragement in theire places, by our not greiving theyre spirites through our Irregularities." [70] If it had not done so earlier, Salem probably at this time adopted the new test for church membership. If so, Cotton's sermon signalized the transformation of the Salem church from a Separatist type of Congregationalism to the type which had been worked out in Massachusetts in 1633 or 1634.

Though Cotton spoke to the people of Salem, his message was doubtless repeated elsewhere to persuade any other Separatists or potential Separatists to fall into line behind the new system. The Massachusetts churches were to be nonseparating, emphasizing faith as the essence of the church; and they were to ensure the presence of faith in their members by a screening process that included narratives of religious experiences. With the law of 1636, Massachusetts had in effect guaranteed, so far as lay within human power, that its churches would exhibit faith. Hence any Separatist movement within the colony, such as that attempted by Williams in 1635, would be the more inexcusable.

The new law was as important politically as religiously, for it altered not only the character of church membership, but the character of freemanship, that is, the right to vote and hold office in the civil government. In 1631, under the leadership of John Winthrop, the General Court

70. Walker, *Creeds and Platforms*, pp. 117–18.
71. E. S. Morgan, *The Puritan Dilemma: The Story of John Winthrop* (Boston, 1958), pp. 84–100; *Records of Massachusetts Bay*, I, 87.
72. Morgan, *Puritan Dilemma*, pp. 101–14. It should be noted, however, that the governor in 1636 was John Haynes who later left for

had opened freemanship to all church members.[71] But at that time church membership was probably still within the grasp of all well-behaved inhabitants who wanted it. With the act of 1636, the General Court in effect confined freemanship to persons who passed the new test for church membership. The fact that this restriction was accomplished after Winthrop had been replaced as governor is perhaps not coincidental, for Winthrop had been ousted partly because he was thought to be too lenient in his administration.[72]

By 1636, then, the new system of church membership may be said to have reached full definition, legal establishment, and coordination with the civil government in Massachusetts. There probably remained a few churches established before that date where it did not take effect. It is doubtful, for example, that it was practiced in the churches of Newbury or Hingham, which had been gathered in 1635.[73] The dislike of Massachusetts leaders for the practice in these towns may, in fact, have helped to provoke the law of 1636. Even after the establishment of the new system, there was some variety in the way that different churches and ministers applied the test. The church was supposed to exercise charity in judging candidates, and some were doubtless more charitable than others. The famous English Puritan divine, Richard Baxter, later complained that the attempt to discern a work of grace in candidates left churches "with no certaine terms of admittance . . . they are as various as are the *opinions* of the Pastor (yea, the people too) and as their severall degrees of charity." [74] Though Baxter was talking

Connecticut, where freemanship was not confined to church members.
73. Miller, *Orthodoxy in Massachusets*, p. 122; Mather, *Magnalia*, book III, p. 146; Lechford, *Plain Dealing*, p. 56; Walker, *Creeds and Platforms*, p. 160.
74. *Correspondence of Baxter and Eliot*, p. 58.

about English churches in 1670 the observation was equally true of New England at any time in the seventeenth century.

In their initial enthusiasm for the new test, however, most Massachusetts churches seem to have applied it so rigorously that they offended one of the greatest ministers among them, Thomas Hooker. This, at least, was the rumor that went back to England after Hooker led his Newtown church from Massachusetts to found Connecticut. One Robert Stansby wrote to Governor Winthrop, April 17, 1637, of the dismay in England over the fact "That you are so strict in admission of members to your church, that more then one halfe are out of your church in all your congregations, and that Mr. Hooker before he went away preached against yt (as one report who hard hym) (and he saith) now although I knowe all must not be admitted yet this may do much hurt. . . ." [75] Cotton Mather, writing at the end of the seventeenth century and seeking to emphasize the attachment of the founding fathers to tests of saving faith, admitted that Hooker was less strict than other early ministers: at Hartford he required no relation of experiences before the church (unless the candidate wished to give one) but examined the candidate privately, in company with the elders, asking "certain probatory Questions." Moreover, says Mather, he was very sparing in the exercise of church discipline and tried to avoid censures and excommunication altogether.[76]

There is evidence that the Hartford church, if more lenient than others, did make some effort to discern faith in its members, for George Wyllys, a member of the church, wrote in 1644 that "with us none are admitted to

75. *Winthrop Papers*, III, 390.
76. *Magnalia*, book III, pp. 66–67. Cf. Miller, *Colony to Province*, pp. 73–74.
77. Connecticut Historical Society, *Collections*, XXI (1924), 68.

partake of the seales of the covenant, but such, and their seed, as in the judgment of charity have truth of grace." [77] But Hooker's judgment was more charitable than that of most other ministers. None was more concerned than Hooker with the generation of saving faith, and none preached or wrote more eloquently about its operation; but Hooker believed that the first signs of it could be detected at an early stage in the morphology of conversion: [78] and his writings confirm Mather's suggestion that he was lenient in admissions. In his *Survey of the Summe of Church Discipline* Hooker maintained that if a man "live not in the commission of any known sin, nor in the neglect of any known duty, and can give a reason of his hope towards God," he was fit for church membership. Agreement to this rule, Hooker said, "would mervailously facilitate the work of *Admission*, without any trouble, and prevent such curious inquisitions and niceties, which the pride and wantonness of mens spirits hath brought into the Church, to disturb the peace thereof, and to prejudice the progresse of God's ordinance." [79] Although Hooker was purportedly defending the New England way against its English critics, these words sound like criticism of a too great severity used in Massachusetts.

If Hooker did indeed advocate and practice a more generous membership policy in Connecticut than prevailed in Massachusetts, the emigration of Dorchester families to Connecticut takes on a new significance. The first settlers of Dorchester had gathered their church in England just before departure and had chosen John Warham as minister.[80] After they arrived in the New World, Deacon Fuller of Plymouth reported conferring until he was weary with

78. See note 58.
79. *Survey of the Summe of Church Discipline* (London, 1648), book III, p. 6.
80. *Chronicles of Massachusetts*, p. 347.

the Reverend Mr. Warham, because the latter believed that "the visible [81] church may consist of a mixed people, godly, and openly ungodly." [82] Warham may have led his flock to Windsor, Connecticut, in 1635 because he did not agree with the newly developed Massachusetts system and preferred to be near Hooker who held views closer to his own. It may be noted also that Connecticut did not follow Massachusetts in making church membership a requirement for freemanship.

The settlers of the New Haven colony, on the other hand, favored both the strict admissions plan of Massachusetts and the restriction of freemanship to church members. John Davenport, the first minister, explained his position on church membership in a pamphlet published in 1663,[83] and Mather tells us that in conducting the New Haven church, Davenport made *"Church Purity* to be one of his greatest Concernments and Endeavors . . . he used a more than ordinary Exactness in Trying, those that were Admitted unto the Communion of the Church: Indeed so very thoroughly, and I had almost said, severely strict, were the Terms of his Communion, and so much, I had well nigh said over-much, were the Golden Snuffers of the Sanctuary employ'd by him in his Exercise of Discipline towards those that were Admitted, that he did all that was possible, to render the Renowned Church of *New Haven,* like the *New Jerusalem.*" [84] After the New Haven colony was annexed to Connecticut in 1662, John Davenport marched back to Boston. Do we have here, in their differing views of church membership and the attendant question of freemanship, one explanation for the coolness

81. In the printed text of Bradford's Letter Book this word is given as "invisible," which is clearly a mistake in copying, but I have been unable to locate the original manuscript. In the quotation as given by the editors of Bradford's *History,* II, 113n, the word is "visible," which is obviously the word intended.

that always existed between Connecticut and the New Haven colony?

While Connecticut seems to have applied the test less strictly and New Haven more strictly than Massachusetts, Rhode Island was settled in large part by persons who wished to carry the new test to an extreme, at the expense of all other qualifications for membership. Roger Williams, during his residence in Massachusetts, was notorious for demanding a greater degree of purity in the church than other New Englanders thought possible or desirable. His demands took many forms, none of which, as recorded, was focused on admission procedures. But after Williams' arrival in Rhode Island, Winthrop, who was in friendly correspondence with him, reported that he reached the point where he thought no one in the world but himself and his wife were fit for church communion.[85] Williams, however, was volatile and ever-changing in his religious opinions.

The main group of emigrants to Rhode Island were followers of Anne Hutchinson. Mrs. Hutchinson was an admirer of John Cotton, and she carried Cotton's insistence on unmerited saving grace far beyond her master, to the point where she ultimately claimed to be in direct communication with the Almighty. Her followers allegedly maintained that God enabled them to tell with absolute certainty whether a man had saving grace or not. They therefore proposed to make their own discernment of this quality the only basis for admission to the church. Understanding of the Scriptures and good behavior were obviously superfluous qualifications if saints could recog-

82. Massachusetts Historical Society, *Collections*, first series, III, 74.
83. *Another Essay for Investigation of the Truth* (Cambridge, 1663).
84. Mather, *Magnalia*, book III, p. 55. Cf. Lechford, *Plain Dealing*, p. 33.
85. Winthrop, *History*, I, 369.

nize one another through some supernatural gift of discernment.[86]

I do not wish to imply that the settlement of Connecticut and Rhode Island were the result simply of a disagreement about the new test for church membership. This was only one element in a complex situation. It is, however, an element that may help us to understand the distinguishing characteristics of the several New England colonies.

It will also help to clarify the relationship and differences between New England Puritans and their English counterparts. The new procedures and the new test for membership in New England had become sufficiently well known by the end of the 1630's to invite the attention of English Puritans, who sent queries about them to the New England ministers. Richard Mather drafted an answer in 1638 or 1639, which was approved by the other ministers, sent over to England, and published there in 1643.[87] Here the new procedures were fully described as they were in later defenses of the New England way by John Cotton, Thomas Hooker, and John Norton, and in a less friendly description by Thomas Lechford.[88] It was also, no doubt, described and defended in many private letters.[89]

As a result, the New England way quickly won adherents in England. With the calling of the Long Parliament in 1641, the opportunity to reform the Church of England was suddenly at hand. But when the Puritans set about the task, they found themselves divided about a number of details. The one that has received most attention from

86. Thomas Weld, *A Short Story of the Rise, reign, and ruin of the Antinomians* (London, 1644), pp. 6, 14; Mather, *Magnalia*, book VII, p. 14.

87. *Church Government and Church Covenant Discussed.*

88. See references in note 45 and also Cotton, *The Way of the Congregational Churches Cleared;* Hooker, *Survey of the Summe of Church Discipline;* and Norton, *The Answer* (1648), trans. Douglas Horton (Cambridge, Mass., 1958).

historians was the question of whether the churches should be united in a presbyterial and synodical organization or whether each church should be independent of the others. To many of the Puritans themselves, however, the question which loomed largest was that of church membership. Those who favored congregational independence also favored the New England method of restricting membership. In arguing against the Independents, the Presbyterians furnished one more testimony to the novelty of the New England practice. Robert Baillie, the most articulate enemy of the Independents, thought that testing the faith of prospective members was the crucial difference that divided Presbyterians from Independents. And while he attacked Independency as the child of separation, he correctly perceived that the two were not identical. The Independents, he said in a passage discussing tests of faith:

much out-runne the *Brownists;* for they [the Brownists] did never offer to separate upon this ground alone; and the matter whereupon here they stumbled, was only open profanenesse and that incorrigible, either through want of power or want of care to remedy it. If the profanenesse was not open and visible, or if the Church had her full power to execute discipline, and according to her power made conscience really to censure scandalls: These things as I conceive, would have abundantly satisfied the *Brownists,* and cured their separation.

But the Independents now doe draw them up much higher then they were wont to stand; they teach them to stumble not only at open profanenesse, but at the want of true grace; yea, at the want of convincing signs of Regeneration.[90]

89. Many are cited in William Rathband, *A Brief Narration of Some Church Courses Held in Opinion and Practise in the Churches lately erected in New England* (London, 1644).

90. Baillie, *Dissuasive*, p. 156. Cf. Rathband, *Brief Narration*, p. 51. On the use by English Congregationalists (after 1640) of narratives of the work of grace, see Nuttall, *Visible Saints*, pp. 109–12.

The quarrel between Presbyterians and Independents in England is beyond the scope of the present investigation, but Baillie's testimony on this point, which is supported by all the surviving evidence, emphasizes for us once again the novelty of what the New England churches were attempting. New England was an effort to reduce the gap between God and man, and the New England churches stood at the farthest outpost that man could reach toward ecclesiastical holiness. They disclaimed as sacrilegious the efforts of an Anne Hutchinson or a Roger Williams to jump the gap entirely, but they hoped to make themselves as pure as humans could. In the 1630's and 40's they seemed to be succeeding, but the world has many ways of defeating those who try to stand too far from it.

- 4 -

The Halfway Covenant

❧

THE ENGLISH emigrants to New England were the first Puritans to restrict membership in the church to visible saints, to persons, that is, who had felt the stirrings of grace in their souls, and who could demonstrate this fact to the satisfaction of other saints. The early Separatists had demanded the exclusion from the church of the visibly wicked; the later Separatists, and especially Henry Ainsworth, had implied that the exclusion of the wicked meant the inclusion only of saints; and at the same time the nonseparating English Puritan divines had been teaching their readers and listeners how to recognize the movements of grace within the soul and thus to determine whether one was a saint or not. It had remained for the New Englanders to combine and carry these ideas to fruition by constructing their churches entirely of persons who had demonstrated their sainthood to one another.

The impulse that produced this development was not novel. It had moved Donatists, Montanists, Albigensians, and many other Christians over the centuries. In the sixteenth and seventeenth centuries it carried the Baptists and the Quakers even farther than the Puritans. It was nothing more than man's yearning for holiness. The church has always been man's way of approaching divinity, and those who have joined the church have often sought to carry it with them in their progress from the wickedness of the world toward the goodness of God. The danger in such a move is seldom apparent to those who make it, the danger of deserting the world in search of a perfection that belongs only to heaven.

Those Puritans who believed in Congregationalism, that is, in churches gathered from the world by free consent, were especially prone to the danger. Although they prided themselves on not seeking perfection, the very act of gathering a church implied a departure from the world and a closer approach to perfection than others had attained. In New England the requirement that members have saving faith moved the churches farther from the world than the Separatist ones in England and Holland, which had required only good behavior and orthodox belief. To be sure, the New England Puritans admitted that their churches inevitably contained bad men as well as good, hypocrites who deceived their brethren and perhaps themselves by false assurance. But no such persons were knowingly tolerated. As Thomas Shepard, the pastor of the church at Cambridge, said, "if we could be so Eagle-eyed, as to discern them now that are Hypocrites, we should exclude them now," for "one man or woman secretly vile, which the Church hath not used all means to discover, may defile a whole Church." [1]

In moving their churches so close to God and so far from the world, the New England Puritans were doing what they believed that God required. But the move created a special difficulty for them, which was closely related to the problem that I have elsewhere called the Puritan dilemma, the problem of doing right in a world that does wrong. In a study of John Winthrop I have

1. *Parable of the Ten Virgins*, II, 197, 198.

tried to show how an individual Puritan met this dilemma
and how it affected his conduct of the civil government
of Massachusetts. John Winthrop, while trying to live as
God required, learned that he must live *in* the world, face
its temptations, and share its guilt; and Winthrop helped
to prevent the government of Massachusetts from seeking
a greater perfection in this world than God required or
allowed.[2]

Winthrop had less control, and less understanding, of
the church than of the state. And the church, by any standards, had to be more pure than the state. But the New England churches, by the mid-1630's, were committed to a
degree of purity that left their relationship with the world
highly uncertain and untried by any previous experience
in England or Europe. If the church could have been truly
gathered from the world into eternity, there would have
been no problem, for in eternity the visible and invisible
churches would have become one. Freed from the world,
and from their own corruptions, the members could have
adored God in perpetual glory. But the visible church,
like man himself, must remain *in* the world and must not
only bring its members closer to God but must also help
to redeem the rest of the world.

It was the church's task, acknowledged by Christians in
all ages, to spread the gospel, to offer to all men the means
of salvation. Though Puritans and other Calvinists thought
the means would be effective only with God's predestined
elect, not even the New England churches could hope to
identify God's elect *before* God made that election manifest in saving faith. Though the New England churches
might accept for membership only those who already had
saving faith, they must offer the means of faith indiscriminately to all, serving as God's instrument for beget-

2. *The Puritan Dilemma.*

ting faith in those who were predestined to receive it but had not yet done so. How to discharge this basic responsibility of the church became an increasingly difficult problem for the New England Puritans as they developed their idea of restricted church membership: their churches must not only be gathered out of the world but must continually gather *in* the world, continually search for new saints.

To the Anglican as to the Roman Catholic Church, this was no problem. With all but the most notorious sinners included, indeed compelled, within the visible church, each man could gain from it whatever God wished him to gain: the saint could grow in grace; the as-yet-unconverted saint could gain the understanding he needed for conversion; and all others could learn the justice of God in damning them. Everyone in the community was perforce exposed to all the means of grace, and there was no need to distinguish one man's eternal condition from another's. But how could a church serve God as an instrument for converting sinners if it consisted only of those who had been converted already?

This problem had faced the first gathered churches of Separatists. Even though they did not pretend to discern saving faith in the religious experiences of their members, they did appear to turn their backs on the mass of sinners around them. The Anglicans and the nonseparating Puritans accused them of neglecting the task of converting sinners and of plucking the fruit of other men's labors, of gathering men and women who had been taught Christianity in the very churches they complained of. How many persons, it was asked, had the Separatists "brought from

3. William Rathband, *A Most Grave and Modest Confutation of the Sect, commonly called Brownists or Separatists* (London, 1644), Preface. Though printed in 1644, this tract was written "many yeares since."

4. Burrage, *Early English Dissenters*, II, 141. Cf. Robinson, *Works*,

grosse ignorance, unto true knowledge, from infidelitie, to holy Faith, from profanesse of life, to a conscionable walking with God?" Whatever understanding or faith the Separatists could lay claim to, they had "received by the ministerie of those men, and in the bosome of those Churches, which now they condemne." [3] In 1618 Thomas Drakes pointed out that "The Apostles, Evangelists, and ther holy successors, converted all sorts unto God, but these refined reformers, onely seduce the sound, and pervert and estrange from us, those, that are otherwise well affected." [4] And in Plymouth in 1624, the Pilgrims were accused of withholding the means of grace from all but the members of the church on the ground that "the Lord hath not appointed any ordinary ministrie for the conversion of those that are without." [5]

To such charges the Separatists could return only the feeblest of answers. They dodged the question of their own guilt by insisting that the business of the ministry was not to convert souls "but to fede and edifie" and discipline those already converted. [6] On this basis they could defend their own churches as true churches in spite of their failure to minister to sinners; and they could simultaneously attack the Anglican church as no church in spite of its conversions of sinners. In this argument and others the Separatists virtually denied the evangelistic function of the church. They even suggested that the government hire talented laymen to convert sinners, not as ministers but simply as preachers or speakers who would instruct the people in parish assemblies. Any who profited by the instruction could then join a church and come under the

II, 54–55.
    5. Bradford, *History*, I, 399. Cf. the Pilgrims' answer to this accusation, *ibid.*, 401–402.
    6. Robinson, *Works*, II, 9–10, 401; Smyth, *Paralleles*, p. 140; Ainsworth, *Counterpoyson*, pp. 11, 69.

care of a true minister.[7] But such a suggestion implied that
someone other than a minister could preach the gospel,
and if so why not the vicars and curates and priests whom
the Separatists denounced? The Separatists were indeed
caught with the old riddle of the chicken and the egg. One
nonseparating Puritan put the question to John Robinson,
as to how on Separatist principles true churches could ever
have been gathered in England after their alleged destruc-
tion by popery:

Nowe, yf egge and bird be distroyed, I meane Church and
ministerye, as you imagine, and the one cannott be without
the other, riddle and tell me which shall be first, and where
we shall beginne, whether at the bird or att the egg, whether
at the ministerye or at the Church? Not at the Church, for
that must be gathered by a ministerye of God's appoyntment,
not at the ministerye, for there can be none but pastors and
teachers, and these cannot exercise a ministerye without a
calling, nor have a calling but from a true Church, which
must not be compelled by the majestrate, but gathered by
doctrine of the word into a voluntarye covenant with God.
If you saie that till the Churches be gathered, there maie be
another ministerye then that of Appostles, prophets, evan-
gelistes, pastors, or teachers, then you confes Christ hath not
taken order for all those kinds of ministeryes which should
be needfull for the gathering together of all the saintes, con-
trarye to Ephe. 4, by your selues alleadged, and that there
maie be some other ministery lawfullye and profitablie used,
then he hath ordeyned, which you denye.

Looke about you well and see that you are wrapped up in
your owne cobweb, and eyther must breake it and lett the
flie goe, or be swept awaie with it and her. Nowe God give
you a wise hearte to consider this well. . . .[8]

7. Smyth, *Paralleles*, p. 111; Barrow, *A Collection of Certain Letters*,
p. 59.
8. Burrage, *Answer to John Robinson*, p. 76. Cf. Barrow, *A Col-*

The riddle was more than a technical difficulty, for it exposed a fatal arrogance at the heart of Separatism. The Separatist churches had no way of redeeming the world, no way of gathering new members except through the labors of other ministers whose mission they refused to recognize. The nonseparating Puritans in England escaped this dilemma and embraced the world of sinners in order to clasp the saints contained within it. They recognized the churches of England as true churches in need of reform but not without hope, and they charged the Separatists with arrogating to themselves an absurd self-righteousness, "as yf," one of them told John Robinson, "God had sent Mr. Johnson and you as the fire from heaven and had on earth no true visible Church rightlie gathered and constituted in his worship but yours at Leyden and his at Amsterdam." [9]

While the nonseparating Puritans remained in England, it must be remembered, they had not yet developed the idea of a church composed exclusively of saints. When they proposed to reform the churches of England, they thought of expelling the visibly wicked, not of regathering the church from persons demonstrating saving faith. (Even in New England, once they admitted a man to church membership, they would expel him only for open wickedness.) Doubtless they would have limited the Lord's Supper to a smaller group within each church, but they would have encompassed the majority of the population as church members and would have excluded or expelled only that part of the world which was in open rebellion against God. It came as a distinct shock to the English Puritans when rumors began to drift across the Atlantic

lection of Certain Letters, pp. 58–59; R. Alison, *A Plaine Confutation of Brownisme* (London, 1590), p. 125.

9. Burrage, *Answer to John Robinson,* p. 79.

in the late 1630's that their New England brethren, who
in England had condemned the exclusiveness of the Separatists, were now practicing an even more invidious exclusiveness themselves.

When they left England in the 1630's, many Puritans
assumed that they could and would leave the bad part of
the world behind. They soon found that they could not.
The fifteen or twenty thousand men and women who dis-
embarked in New England between 1630 and 1640 included large numbers who had to be classified as visibly
wicked, so many indeed that some of the founders contemplated a further withdrawal to an isolated area from
which this "mixed multitude" should be excluded. The
wisest recognized that the world neither could nor should
be left behind, and no further exodus occurred. But in the
1630's, by adopting the new strict view of church membership, the New England Puritans executed a spiritual
withdrawal from the mixed multitude that amounted almost to an ecclesiastical abdication from the world. They
failed to consider, before adopting the new standards of
membership, what relation their churches should bear to
the mass of men excluded by those standards, and their
failure exposed them to even more serious charges of neglect and arrogance than they themselves had formerly
made against the Separatists.

Outside the church in New England stood not only the
mixed multitude of wicked Englishmen and heathen natives, but also the visibly good, who understood and believed the doctrines of Christianity and lived accordingly
but who lacked the final experience of grace. The New
England churches made no differentiation among these
seemingly different men. Indeed the New England ministers devoted a good deal of time to showing that there
was no difference in the eyes of God between the vilest

sinner and the "civil" man, who obeyed God's commands outwardly but did not love God in his heart.[10] The only distinction among men in the eyes of God was between those who had saving faith and those who lacked it. Therefore the civil and the uncivil alike were kept outside God's church.

Outside the church in New England, moreover, a man was much farther removed from most of the means of grace than he would have been in the Old World. In England and Holland the establishment of Separatist churches had deprived no one of church membership, for the Separatists were surrounded by other, more comprehensive churches open to all. In New England the Puritans, certain that their way was the only one, forbade the erection of other churches. If a man could not qualify as a visible saint, he was wholly outside any church. He could not be baptized. He could not have his children baptized. He could not take communion. In England both these ordinances were available to everyone and were widely believed to be means of conversion through which God acted on the individual just as He did through preaching of the Gospel. But the New England Puritans did not share this belief and therefore felt obliged to deny baptism and communion to the unconverted. In their view both ordinances were seals of the covenant of grace which God extended to his elect. To permit an unbeliever to participate in them would be blasphemous. By this exclusion, however, the church deprived itself of two traditional means of bringing unregenerate men closer to God.

Church discipline, which might also have served this purpose, was similarly confined to those who least needed

10. See, for example, Thomas Hooker, *The Christians Two Chiefe Lessons* (London, 1640), p. 213; Thomas Shepard, *Works*, ed. John Albro (3 vols.; Boston, 1853), I, 29.

it. It was used only for recovering or expelling backsliding members. In England, though church discipline was lax, everyone in the community was subject to it. But the New England Puritans assigned to the state the task of disciplining those whom they excluded from their churches.

The absence of ties between the unregenerate part of the community and the church gave the latter an unprecedented purity, but it also placed the very life of the church in jeopardy. The members of the New England churches had themselves come from imperfect churches, in which they had learned the doctrines of Christianity, had taken the sacraments, and received the experience of grace that qualified them for membership in the proper churches of New England. But how would the mass of men who had come to New England unqualified for membership ever become qualified? How would civil men be encouraged to persevere in their outward obedience in the hope of eventual faith? How would the wicked be shown their wickedness? How would the gospel be spread to the heathen? Before leaving for America, many Puritan spokesmen had affirmed a desire to convert the natives. How would they do it with a church designed only for the saved? Without a surrounding of imperfect, unreformed churches, where would the reformed ones obtain a supply of members? How would God's elect be plucked from the mixed multitude?

New Englanders had failed to consider these questions, and when English Puritans asked them, the New Englanders, like the Separatists before them, replied in terms that exposed their failure to recognize the church's mission in the world. John Cotton, for example, the principal spokes-

11. *The Way of the Congregational Churches Cleared*, p. 74.

12. *Records of the Massachusetts Bay Company*, III, 99.

13. *Records of the Colony or Jurisdiction of New Haven, from May, 1653, to the Union*, ed. C. J. Hoadly (Hartford, 1858), p. 588; *The*

man for the New England way, could only ask of his critics: "May there not fall out to be Hypocrites in our Flock? and must wee not preach for their conversion? And are not the children of the Members of our Church, many of them such, as when they grow up stand in need of converting grace? . . . Besides when an Indian or unbeleever commeth into the Church, doe not all the prophets that preach the Word . . . apply their speech to his conviction and conversion?" [11]

The honest answer to the last of these questions was probably no. Nevertheless the New England Puritans did take one measure to fulfill the church's evangelical mission. Instead of waiting for unbelievers to wander into the meetinghouse, the civil government of Massachusetts in 1646 passed a law requiring everyone within a town to attend the preaching of the word.[12] Such laws were also passed in the New Haven and Connecticut colonies.[13] The government undoubtedly hoped that compulsory church attendance would improve the colonists not only in godliness but in behavior. Whether the result matched the hope is questionable, for those who attended from compulsion were unlikely to derive from the experience any feeling of kinship to the church. New England preaching, from the point of view of the unregenerate, left much to be desired. Although the Puritans acknowledged preaching to be the principal means through which God converted men, ministers addressed themselves more to saints than to sinners, in sermons designed less to plant the seed of faith than to nourish it where it already grew.[14]

To be sure, not all ministers neglected the unregenerate. Some preachers undoubtedly tried to make new converts

Public Records of the Colony of Connecticut, Prior to the Union with New Haven Colony, ed. J. Hammond Trumbull (Hartford, 1850), p. 524.

14. E. S. Morgan, *The Puritan Family* (Boston, 1944, 1956), pp. 90–104.

from their captive audiences. The surviving sermons of Thomas Hooker, for example, are often addressed to perishing sinners. A few ministers like John Eliot even devoted their spare time to converting the Indians. But for the most part the New England churches, in striving for purity of membership, neglected sinners and heathen and civil men to concentrate on the advancement in grace of those who had already demonstrated saving faith.

If a New Englander did pause to consider the sinners outside the church, he was likely to compromise his insistence on purity of membership. John Eliot, for example, in corresponding with English Puritans about the church's evangelical mission, found himself proposing measures that were inconsistent with New England practice. At one point he advocated admitting everyone in a congregation to the privileges of the church "so as to keep the whole heape of chaff and corne together, only excluding the ignorant and prophane and scandalous." From this undifferentiated mass, there might be simultaneously gathered a special group of "the holy Saints, who are called higher by the grace of Christ," and who might "injoy together a more strickt and select communion" without deserting the regular parochial communion.[15] At another time Eliot proposed transplanting the holiest members of outstanding congregations into other congregations which needed some shining examples to leaven the wicked in their midst.[16]

Eliot never attempted to carry out these novel proposals which he made to Richard Baxter as suggestions for the churches of England. In New England, he and other Puritan ministers continued to exclude from the sacraments all but the proven regenerate. In spite of prodding from English Presbyterians and Anglicans, the New Englanders re-

15. *Correspondence of Baxter and Eliot*, p. 25. Cf. John Eliot, *Communion of Churches* (Cambridge, Mass., 1665).

fused to reverse their withdrawal from the world, and
refused any accommodation within the church to the
well meaning and well behaved. But the world has its
own ways of controlling those who propel themselves too
far from it; and the New England churches were eventually brought back to earth, not by the corruptions of
the flesh, but by its biology.

The way of the world even in Massachusetts was to be
born, grow old, and die. In the process each generation
had to beget the next; and children did not spring full-
grown and fully educated from their mothers' wombs.
They had to be nursed and nurtured mentally and spirit-
ually as well as physically until they were fit to stand by
themselves. Somehow the organization of the church had
to be accommodated to these facts of life. As the saints
died and their children grew up, there had to be a way
of getting the new generation into the church.

The Baptists, with a yearning for purity similar to that
of the Puritans, solved the problem, or succeeded in ignor-
ing it, by recruiting all new members from adult Christians who had been awakened by Baptist preaching or the
preaching of other ministers. As old believers died, newly
converted ones would take their places; children were incapable of any kind of membership. The Puritans, both
Separatist and non-Separatist, had disclaimed "Anabap-
tism." Although the most ardent sometimes succumbed to
its attractions, the great majority believed that God required the church to baptize not only converted saints
previously unbaptized but also the children of saints. Such
children became members of the church, but not in the
same sense as their parents.

In what sense was a question that troubled the Separatists in England and Holland very little. The younger

16. *Correspondence of Baxter and Eliot*, p. 40.

children of Separatist church members there did not participate in the Lord's Supper, but as they grew to maturity, they could easily qualify for all the privileges of the church, if they wished to, simply by behaving themselves and learning what they were taught. But the Separatist experience could offer no assistance to New Englanders in this matter. New England had prescribed not merely understanding and good behavior but an experience of conversion, an experience beyond the range of human volition, as a qualification for adult membership. Yet New England still admitted children to this church by baptism, apparently expecting that they would pass from child membership to adult membership when they grew up, just as they had done in the Separatist churches and in the Church of England.[17] It was an arrogant and inconsistent expectation, for it implied a presumption that every child of a saint was destined for salvation and such a presumption was obviously wrong. No Christian could believe that grace was really hereditary.

The Puritans tried to overcome this inconsistency by demanding that when the child of a saint grew up he must demonstrate to the church that he was indeed saved. Until he did so, by the same kind of examination that adults seeking membership were subjected to, he should not be admitted to the Lord's Supper. So said John Cotton, Richard Mather, and the synod of divines who between 1646 and 1648 drafted the exposition of Puritan beliefs and practices which is usually referred to as the Cambridge Platform.[18] But the men who framed the Cambridge Platform did not say what happened to the membership of a child if he grew up and did not experience faith.

17. The founders of the Salem church evidently shared the Separatists' expectation that the ensuing generations would enter the church as they acquired an adult understanding of the principles of religion. See Morton, *New Englands Memoriall*, p. 77.

Before two decades had passed, the fact was plain that most children of saints did not receive saving faith by the time they were physically mature. To judge from surviving records, it was uncommon for a man or woman to have the requisite religious experience before he was in his twenties. Often it came much later, and many otherwise good men and women never received it.

But if the holy spirit reached these men and women late or not at all, biological urges reached them early. They married young and had large families. When an unconverted child of a church member produced a child of his own, the minister of his church was presented with a problem, the complexity of which had not been foreseen by the architects of the New England system. The new father (or mother) had been in some sense a member of the church. Was he still? If so, was he a member in a different sense than before? What about the child? Was the child a member? Should the child be baptized?

The questions were difficult to answer, because every answer generated several more questions. If a child who grew to physical maturity without receiving faith was to be considered no longer a member of the church, how and when should his expulsion take place? The fact that he had acquired a child before he acquired faith was no sign that he would not eventually attain faith. Should the church meanwhile cast him out? If so, upon what grounds could it be done? The New Englanders, in adopting the new standard of membership, had not correspondingly altered their conception of church discipline. Admonitions and excommunications were still applied only for misconduct or for openly expressed heretical ideas; no one suggested that anyone be excommunicated for failure to dis-

18. Cotton, *The Way of the Congregational Churches Cleared*, pp. 5, 79–80, 111–13; Mather, *Church Government and Church Covenant Discussed*, pp. 20–22; Walker, *Creeds and Platforms*, p. 224.

play signs of saving faith. When, therefore, a child of a member grew to maturity without faith but without misconduct, it was impossible to find grounds for expelling him. To excommunicate him for having a child in lawful wedlock was palpably absurd. On the other hand, if he remained a member, his child must be entitled to baptism, and if so, why not that child's child too, and so on until the church should cease to be a company of the faithful and should become a genealogical society of the descendants of the faithful.

The Puritans had in fact moved the church so far from the world that it would no longer fit the biological facts of life. Had they been willing to move it a little farther still, by forming monasteries instead of churches, they might have concentrated on their own purity and left to others the task of supplying the church with new members. Had they been willing to abandon infant baptism, they might at least have avoided the embarrassment of trying to adjust spiritual growth to physical. As it was, they had chosen to apply in time and space a conception of the church that could never fit those dimensions. Given both infant baptism and the restriction of church membership to visible saints, it was impossible for the Puritans either to evade the questions just posed or to answer them without an elaborate casuistry that bred dissatisfaction and dis-

19. The surviving records are not clear on this matter, but the controversial literature following the synod of 1662 seems to support this statement. Jonathan Mitchel charged the opponents of the synod with holding principles that would require the expulsion of "all the adult Children of our Churches that are not come up to full Communion." The implication is that such expulsions had not taken place and would be shocking if they did. (*A Defence of the Answer*, pp. 4–16.) Richard Mather implies that the churches had not generally exercised discipline toward adult children of members: ". . . we know but little of the exercise of Church-discipline towards such." (*Ibid.*, p. 60.) Increase Mather in *A Discourse Concerning the Subject of Baptisme* (Cambridge, Mass., 1675) states (p. 29) that churches in Plymouth colony exercised discipline toward children of the church, but (pp. 30–32) that elsewhere it was neglected. But perhaps these statements all refer to ex-

agreement. The history of the New England churches during the seventeenth and eighteenth centuries was in large measure a history of these dissatisfactions and disagreements.

In the first decade after the establishment of the more rigorous standard of membership, the questions were not yet urgent. The older children of church members in the new churches had been baptized in England and were perhaps not considered as sharing in their parents' membership. By the late 1640's, however, an increasing number of children who had been baptized in New England churches were coming of age without a religious experience and starting families of their own. The synod which met at Cambridge in 1646–1648 had been asked to decide the status of these persons. Since it failed to do so, every church during the 1650's had to face the question for itself, and most of them seem to have adopted a do-nothing policy by neither expelling the second-generation adults nor baptizing their third-generation children.[19]

By the late 1650's, the preaching of the word was generating few conversions, and with the end of the Great Migration, the overseas supply of saints had been cut off. As the first generation of Puritans died, the churches declined rapidly in membership, and it appeared that a majority of the population would soon be unbaptized.[20] This

communication rather than lesser forms of discipline, for Henry Dunster in a letter written about 1652, stated concerning unconverted children of members: ". . . such there be amongst us with whom the Church bears patiently, using means for their Conviction and Conversion. And in case they break out into any unchristian courses, admonish them, and if they continue in them, wholy withdraw from them. But I have not knowne any of these formally excommunicated because they neither cared for nor sought Communion." Jeremiah Chaplin, *Life of Henry Dunster* (Boston, 1872), p. 288.

20. "It is easie to see that in the way your self and some others go, *the bigger half of the people in this Country will in a little Time be unbaptized.*" Jonathan Mitchel to Increase Mather, appended to Increase Mather, *The First Principles of New England* (Cambridge, Mass., 1675).

was an alarming situation for a community which had been founded for religious purposes. It was one thing to create a church of saints; it was another to let those saints carry the church out of the world with them entirely when they died. A meeting of ministers in 1657 and a full-scale synod in 1662 considered the problem and tried to find a solution that would retain a pure membership without destroying the church.

The synod did not address itself to the fundamental problem of the church's relation to the world at large, the problem of how to convert the unconverted. Instead, it confined itself to the more limited question posed by the birth of children to baptized persons who had not or not yet received saving faith. The synod adopted seven propositions, most of which simply affirmed the prevailing New England ideas about infant baptism and the construction of churches from visible saints. But the third, fourth, and fifth propositions settled the problem of the unconverted members and their children, as follows:

Proposition 3d. The Infant-seed of confederate visible Believers, are members of the same Church with their parents, and when grown up, are personally under the Watch, Discipline and Government of that Church.

Proposition 4th. These Adult persons are not therefore to be admitted to full Communion, meerly because they are and continue members, without such further qualifications, as the Word of God requireth thereunto.

Proposition 5th. Church-members who were admitted in minority, understanding the Doctrine of Faith, and publickly professing their assent thereto; not scandalous in life, and solemnly owning the Covenant before the Church, wherein they give up themselves and their Children to the Lord, and subject themselves to the Government of Christ in the Church, their Children are to be Baptized.[21]

21. Walker, *Creeds and Platforms*, pp. 325–28.

The fifth proposition was the crucial one. It meant that if a person born and baptized in the church did not receive faith he could still continue his membership and have his own children baptized, by leading a life free of scandal, by learning and professing the doctrines of Christianity, and by making a voluntary submission to God and His church. This submission, which proposition five calls "owning" the covenant, involved acknowledging the covenant with Christ and the church that had been made for one in infancy by one's parents, acknowledging, that is, so far as it lay within human power to do so. Although Puritan theology made such an acknowledgment meaningless unless it was the product of saving faith, owning the covenant was not intended to imply the genuine participation in the covenant of grace that came from saving faith. Nor was "understanding the Doctrine of Faith" supposed to imply the actual possession of faith. All the actions prescribed by the fifth proposition could be performed without saving faith. All were designed for the well-meaning, well-behaved but faithless offspring of the faithful. By the fifth proposition, these persons could retain their membership in the pure churches of New England simply by fulfilling the conditions which had formerly been required for membership in the Separatist churches of England and Holland.

The membership they retained, however, was not the full membership that had been granted in the Separatist churches. Rather it was the continuation of the membership they had had as children: they could not vote in church affairs, and they could not participate in the Lord's Supper (they were not members in "full communion"). What they gained was two privileges which had probably been hitherto denied them in most New England churches: the application of church discipline (they could be admonished or excommunicated for bad conduct) and baptism for their children. They were "half-way" members, and the synod's whole solution to the question of their status was dubbed the "half-way covenant."

The term was one of derision, invented by those who thought the synod's solution constituted a lowering of standards. But these opponents of the synod, who were numerous, proposed an absurd alternative to the concept of halfway membership. Faced with the problem of deciding on the status of the adults whom the synod made halfway members, the opponents admitted that the persons whom the synod placed in this category had been members of the church in their minority and also that they were subject to censure and admonition (but not excommunication) when they became adult. Yet, the opponents held, these persons at some undefined point, without action either by themselves or by the church, ceased to be members. They were "*felos de se*," who cast themselves out of the church. Although the New England churches had never admitted the right of a church member to leave a church unless excommunicated or formally dismissed to another church, grown children were now held to have departed from the church without either themselves or the church knowing it.[22]

Such a view carried the church even farther from the world than the position it had taken in the 1630's. To be sure, the development of restricted membership, from the first Separatists onward, had steadily proceeded toward a greater withdrawal of the church from the world, and this had been accomplished by a continual refinement of doctrine. But the extreme position taken by the opponents of the synod was neither refined nor rational; and most of

22. Charles Chauncy, *Anti-Synodalia Scripta Americana* ([London], 1662); John Davenport, *Another Essay for Investigation of the Truth*

those who took it must eventually have either retreated to the halfway covenant or moved on to repudiate infant baptism.

The halfway covenant, while wholly insufficient as a recognition of the church's relationship to the world, was probably the most satisfactory way of reconciling the Puritans' conflicting commitments to infant baptism and to a church composed exclusively of saints. Its advocates argued persuasively against their opponents that the establishment of halfway membership was the only way in the long run to preserve the purity of full membership. Unless there was such a category the prospect of declining membership and the desire of parents to have their children baptized might tempt churches to admit persons to membership who were unworthy of the Lord's Supper. Men and women would be encouraged to play the hypocrite or to imagine themselves converted, by a process of wishful thinking, in order to gain baptism for their children. Only by distinguishing between those worthy of baptism and those worthy of the Lord's Supper, could the latter be preserved for the truly faithful.[23]

Baptism, it was pointed out, had never been considered as exclusive a sacrament as the Lord's Supper, for Puritans had always recognized baptism in any church, even the Roman Catholic, as valid, and did not repeat the rite for persons converted from that or any other Christian denomination. The drive toward exclusive membership had always aimed primarily at excluding the unworthy from the Lord's Supper. By establishing a category of halfway members, worthy of baptism, the synod hoped to preserve the sanctity of the Lord's Supper.

The supporters of the synod were able to collect a large

(Cambridge, Mass., 1663).
23. Jonathan Mitchel and Richard Mather, *A Defence of the Answer*, pp. 45–46; Increase Mather, *Discourse Concerning Baptisme*, p. 52.

number of testimonies from the books and manuscripts of
the founding fathers, to show that insofar as the fathers
considered the problem they had felt the same way about
it as the synod. Thomas Shepard, Jr., unearthed and published a manuscript by his father, written three months before the latter's death in 1649. In it the elder Shepard, en-
gaging in the familiar Puritan art of making distinctions,
differentiated between the "inward reall holyness" of true
saints and "federal holyness, whether externally professed
as in grown persons, or graciously promised unto their
seed." Only federal holiness was necessary for church
membership. The children of saints must be presumed to
have this and must be considered as church members until
cast out by formal act of the church. Moreover, they must
be cast out only if they committed open, outward offenses
serious enough to bring the same judgment on any other
member who committed them. Shepard, who had once
warned against tolerating any known hypocrite in the
church, was not dismayed in 1649 by a church in which
the majority of members were unregenerate or as yet unregenerate children and children's children. Such a church,
he acknowledged, would contain "many chaffy hypocrites
and oft times prophane persons." But the same, he said,
was true of a church freshly gathered of visible saints: you
could never keep out hypocrites.[24]

Increase Mather, who liked to remind people that he
was the son of Richard Mather and the son-in-law of John
Cotton, at first opposed the halfway covenant. But when
he swung round to support it, he produced an abundance
of manuscripts from the desks of his father and father-in-
law to show that they and their colleagues would have
supported it too. Some of the statements adduced by In-

24. Thomas Shepard, *The Church Membership of Children, and
their Right to Baptisme* (Cambridge, Mass., 1663) pp. 13–14.

crease Mather may have antedated the full development of the New England system, but there were plenty of later ones to show that when the problem arose, the founders were disposed toward the solution adopted by the synod. Richard Mather, for example, in a letter dated in 1651, had stated his opinion "that the Children of *Church members* submitting themselves to the *Discipline of Christ in the Church*, by an act of their own, when they are grown up to mens and womens Estate, ought to be *watched* over as other *members*, and to have their Infants baptized, but themselves not to be received to the *Lords Table*, nor to *voting* in the *Church*, till by the manifestation of *Faith* and *Repentance*, they shall approve themselves to be fit for the same." Mather had admitted, however, in the same letter, that his church had "not yet thus practiced." [25]

The opponents of the synod did have one founding father on their side: John Davenport of New Haven was still alive and could speak for himself. He was the most articulate and strenuous enemy of the halfway covenant, but his opposition was not as damaging as it might have been because there was published proof that during New England's founding years he had held different views. As a candidate for the ministry in the English church at Amsterdam, Davenport had insisted that he would not baptize all infants presented to him but only those presented by their parents, and then only if the parents submitted to an examination about their beliefs or status. In a lengthy defense of this position printed in 1636 he had explained what he demanded of a parent, and that was simply membership in a Christian church (the Anglican church would do) or profession of the Christian faith. Thus in 1636 he had himself demanded much less than the synod demanded in 1662,

25. Increase Mather, *The First Principles of New England*, pp. 10–11.

and as a result he was not in a strong position to accuse the synod of betraying the standards of the founders.[26]

Although the theological battles of the 1660's were frequently waged with ammunition from the writings of the founding fathers, actually neither Davenport nor the other founders of New England had fully considered the problem of the next generation when in the 1630's they had adopted the test of saving faith for membership. And though historians have followed the opponents of the halfway covenant in hailing it as a betrayal of earlier standards and hence a symptom of the decline of piety, it was no such thing — unless John Calvin, Henry Barrow, Henry Ainsworth, John Robinson, William Perkins, William Ames, and William Bradshaw were all inferior in piety to the minority of New England divines in the 1660's who opposed the measure, unless John Davenport in 1636 was inferior in piety to John Davenport in 1664, unless indeed the founders of New England showed more piety by not facing the problem than their successors did by facing and answering it in 1662.

New England piety may have been declining, but the halfway covenant was *not* a symptom of decline. Rather it was an attempt to answer questions which neither English Puritans nor Separatists had had to face, questions which were created by New England's rigorous new conception of church membership but which the originators of that concept, during their brief experience, had generally been able to evade. By the 1660's the questions could no longer be evaded, but if the clergy and members of the New England churches had really been less pious than their predecessors, those questions might never have arisen. If, for example, they had succumbed to Arminianism, it would have been possible for anyone who wished to do so

26. John Davenport, *An Apologeticall Reply to a booke Called An*

to join the church, simply by affirming his possession of a faith that lay within the reach of human volition. The halfway covenant became necessary, because New England churches of the second generation did hold to the standards of the first, because they did retain the belief in infant baptism, and because they did insist on the pattern of conversion outlined by Perkins and Hildersam and Ames.

Whether there was a decline of piety in the population at large is another question entirely, for the halfway covenant had nothing to do with the population at large. It is not a question I am prepared to settle, but it may be worth pointing out that though the rate of conversions during the second and third decades of New England's history was probably much lower than the founders had anticipated, this was not necessarily a sign of a decline in piety. The bulk of the population had arrived during the Great Migration of the 1630's and probably a large number of the first church members became so before the new admissions system was completely set up. How many would have become members if they had had to pass the new test we cannot tell. Since the second generation of New Englanders was thus actually the first generation in which every church member did have to pass the new test, a comparison of membership statistics in the first few decades, if they were available, would not solve our problem.

The halfway covenant, I would maintain then, was neither a sign of decline in piety nor a betrayal of the standards of the founding fathers, but an honest attempt to rescue the concept of a church of visible saints from the tangle of problems created in time by human reproduction. Nevertheless, the halfway covenant does mark the end of a phase in Puritan church history during which

Answer to the unjust complaint of W. B. (Rotterdam, 1636); *Another Essay for Investigation of the Truth* (Cambridge, Mass., 1663).

ministers and church members were so dazzled by the pure new institution they had succeeded in creating that they were for the moment blinded to their obligations to the rest of New England and to the world. The halfway covenant, taken by itself, was a narrow tribal way of recruiting saints, for it wholly neglected the church's evangelical mission to perishing sinners outside the families of its members. But it did turn attention, in however limited a manner, to the problem of propagating the church. As Jonathan Mitchel said, in defending the synod of 1662, "The Lord hath not set up Churches onely that *a few old Christians* may keep one another warm while they live, and then carry away the Church into the cold grave with them when they dye: no, but that they might, with all the care, and with all the Obligations, and Advantages to that care that may be, *nurse up* still successively *another Generation* of Subjects to Christ that may stand up in his *Kingdome* when they are gone, that so he might have a People and Kingdome *successively* continued to him from one Generation to another." [27] With the New England churches' recognition of this obligation, the Puritans' single-minded march toward purity came to rest.

The halfway covenant brought into the open the difficulties that had been lurking in the Puritan conception of church membership from the beginning. From the time when the first Separatists left the Church of England until the establishment in Massachusetts of tests for saving faith, that conception had developed toward making the visible church a closer and closer approximation of the invisible. With the halfway covenant the Puritans recognized that they had pushed their churches to the outer limits of visibility; and the history of the idea we have been tracing reached, if not a stop, at least a turning point.

27. *Defence of the Answer*, p. 45.

- 5 -

Full Circle

❧❀❧

THE HALFWAY COVENANT enabled the Puritans to keep
within the church a number of persons who might otherwise have fallen out of it into the world. But the decision
to keep them inside the church was dictated, in part at least,
by a recognition of the church's errand in the world, by
a willingness to think a little more about the need to gather
members and a little less about those already gathered.

If, however, the recognition had gone no farther than
the synod of 1662 was willing to go, the New England
churches might still have been destroyed by the very zeal
for purity that had created them. If in the search for pure
members, they had looked no farther than the firesides of
the faithful, they would ultimately have succumbed totally
to the tribal devotion to their own offspring that was all
too evident in much Puritan thought.[1] But in the years after
1662 some New Englanders began to turn their attention
more directly to the church's evangelistic functions.

One of the first signs of the new trend was an action of
the governor and council of Massachusetts in 1669. These
magistrates had been reading the Declaration of Faith
adopted by a meeting of English Congregationalists at the
Savoy Palace in London in 1658. The Savoy meeting, in

1. Morgan, *The Puritan Family*, pp. 90–104.

its definition of church polity, had been guided by the New England way, but English Congregationalists had shown a greater sense of evangelism than their New England counterparts. In describing a minister's relation to his church the Savoy Declaration acknowledged that ministers were not obliged to offer the sacraments to any but members, but it went on to say, "yet ought they not to neglect others living within their Parochial Bounds, but besides their constant publique Preaching to them, they ought to enquire after their profiting by the Word, instructing them in, and pressing upon them (whether young or old) the great Doctrines of the Gospel, even personally and particularly, so far as their strength and time will admit." [2]

The governor and council of Massachusetts, considering these words in 1669, thought them appropriate to the situation of New England. In a printed message "to the Elders and Ministers of every Town," they recited the passage and suggested that too many New England ministers were neglecting the nonmembers in their towns. The message continued:

We do therefore think it our duty to emit this Declaration unto you, earnestly desiring, and in the bowels of our Lord Jesus requiring you to be very diligent and careful to Catechize and Instruct all the people (especially the Youth) under your Charge, in the Sound and Orthodox Principles of Christian Religion; and that not onely in publick, but privately from house to house, as blessed *Paul* did, Acts 20.20 or at least three, four, or more Families meeting together, as strength and time may permit, taking to your assistance such godly and grave persons as to you may seem most expedient. And also that you labour to inform your selves (as much as may be meet) how your Hearers do profit by the Word of God, and how their Conversations do agree therewith, and whether the

2. Walker, *Creeds and Platforms*, p. 405.

Youth are taught to Reade the *English* Tongue: taking all occasions to apply suitable *Exhortations* unto them, for the Rebuke of those that do evil, and for the Encouragement of them that do well.

The effectual and constant prosecution hereof, we hope will have a tendency to promote the Salvation of Souls, To suppress the growth of Sin and Prophaneness, to beget more Love and Unity amongst the people and more Reverence and Esteem of the Ministry, and will assuredly be to the enlargement of your Crown and Recompence in Eternal Glory.[3]

It is impossible to tell how far the ministers of Massachusetts carried out the magistrates' recommendation. But the recommendation itself reflected a change in Puritan thinking which facilitated the growth of a more comprehensive policy of church membership: the recommendation implied that a minister had functions extending beyond the persons (members only) who elected him to office. This was a broader conception of the role of the ministry than had generally prevailed in New England's earlier years, when the stress was on the minister's ties with the individual church to which he was joined by covenant. Early Congregationalism had held that a church could exist without a minister (the Plymouth church demonstrated the proposition from 1620 to 1629) and could choose and ordain one without outside assistance, that a minister could not administer the sacraments except to members of his own church, and that he ceased to be a minister if dismissed by his church.

Some New England Puritans had challenged some of these views from the beginning. But in the latter part of the seventeenth century a movement is apparent toward an enlarged view of the minister's functions and authority. The movement is apparent not only in the magistrates'

3. *To the Elders and Ministers of every Town.* Broadside (1669).

recommendation but in the spread after 1690 of ministerial associations, in which the ministers of an area met regularly to consult on common problems.[4] It is apparent in a growing opinion that councils of churches and associations of ministers should enjoy some degree of authority beyond the mere offering of advice.[5] It is apparent in recommendations by ministers that the civil government take steps to ensure the establishment of ministers in every town, with the implication that the existence of a church might depend on the provision of a proper minister.[6] New England ministers continued to regard election by a church as essential to their calling, but they began to take a higher view of their office and to think that a minister, once ordained, had duties unrelated to his church and extending beyond any particular church.

Such ideas might have been regarded in the 1640's or 1650's as leaning too much toward Presbyterianism, for Presbyterians were distinguished from Congregationalists by a more comprehensive conception of both church and ministry. But as Congregationalists began to take more notice of the world, they inevitably found that the barrier separating them from Presbyterians was less formidable than it had appeared to be in England in the 1640's and 1650's. After the restoration of the monarchy in 1660 and with it of episcopacy, Presbyterians and Congregationalists in England were drawn together by their common exclusion from the Church of England. Each party therefore tried to formulate its principles so as to accommodate, insofar as possible, the other. This disposition affected New Englanders too, especially after the loss of the Massachusetts charter was followed by the Dominion of New Eng-

4. Walker, *Creeds and Platforms*, pp. 466–72; Miller, *Colony to Province*, pp. 216, 257–68.
5. Walker, *Creeds and Platforms*, pp. 471–72.
6. Thomas Walley, *Balm in Gilead* (Cambridge, Mass., 1669), pp.

land and the establishment of an Anglican church in Boston. Increase Mather, who was in England during the revolution of 1688, actually took the lead in one attempt to achieve a union, and New England ministers, generally, began to regard their office in more Presbyterian terms.[7]

Historically the magnification of the minister's office has often gone hand-in-hand with a comprehensive policy of church membership, while a limited membership, emphasizing purity, has been associated with a restriction of clerical authority. Where laymen form a church by a freely entered agreement and then create a minister, that minister is likely to direct himself toward serving those who chose him. Though he and they may recognize an obligation to the rest of the world, it is likely to remain secondary and undefined. But as ministers become independent of the laity, they tend to magnify the importance of their own role in the process of redemption and to feel a keener obligation to the unconverted. The clergy of New England followed this pattern. Although the magistrates' recommendation in 1669 suggested only that ministers extend themselves to the nonchurch-members in their towns by preaching and pastoral visits, a substantial number of ministers began in the 1670's or 1680's to make more drastic overtures to the world by offering one or both sacraments to all well-behaved professing Christians.

With regard to the sacrament of baptism, the development of a more liberal policy is difficult to trace. Once the controversy over the synod of 1662 subsided, New Englanders appeared to have settled the question of baptism, for it figured little in the controversial literature of the next few decades. New England opinion on the subject

13–14; Increase Mather, *A Call from Heaven to the Present and Succeeding Generations* (Boston, 1679), p. 74.

7. Walker, *Creeds and Platforms,* pp. 440–62; Miller, *Colony to Province,* pp. 215–18.

was, nevertheless, silently changing. Increase Mather, who had initially opposed the synod's extension of baptism and its institution of halfway membership, had by 1675 become its advocate, and before the end of the century he had decided to extend baptism and halfway membership far more widely than the synod had proposed. In promoting the union of Congregational and Presbyterian churches in London in 1690 and 1691, Mather had agreed to a definition of church membership as including "such persons as are knowing and sound in the *fundamental Doctrines of the Christian Religion,* without Scandal in their Lives; and to a Judgment regulated by the Word of God, are persons of visible Godliness and Honesty; credibly professing cordial subjection to Jesus Christ." [8] Though Increase Mather and his son Cotton interpreted this statement so as still to require a work of saving grace for participation in the Lord's Supper, they both extended baptism to all professing Christians of good behavior. Cotton Mather, in advocating the principles of the union, emphasized that *"Persons* may be *Disciples,* while they are not yet Risen to the more Experienced state of *Brethren;* and there may be *Subjects* in the *Kingdom,* which have not yet all the Priviledges that the Members of the *Corporations* lay claim unto: now *Baptism* should belong sure, to all the *Disciples* and *Subjects* of our Lord. From a *Nursery* thus watered with *Baptism,* our Churches may be supply'd, from time to time, and multitudes of well-disposed People who by Doubts and Fears are for a while discouraged from the *Lords Table* may thus be kept under *Engagements to be the Lords."* [9]

Although the absence of full records makes it impossible

8. Walker, *Creeds and Platforms,* p. 457.
9. Cotton Mather, *Blessed Unions* (Boston, 1692), p. 71.
10. Cotton Mather, *Thirty Important Cases Resolved* (Boston, 1699), p. 70.

to determine the practice of most churches at any particular point, the Mathers were certainly not alone in their new comprehensiveness. In 1699 the ministers from neighboring churches met at Cambridge and resolved "That such as do profess the True *Christian Religion,* and do not by any *Fundamental Error* in Doctrine, or by a *Scandalous Conversation* contradict that Profession; They and their Children, do belong unto the *Visible Church* and have Right unto *Baptism;* Whether they be Joyned in Fellowship, with a *Particular Church*, or not." [10]

This position evidently represented a trend, for by 1726 Cotton Mather could claim that "there is not one Person in all the Country [New England] free from a scandalous and notorious disqualifying *Ignorance* and *Impiety*, but what may repair to some Hundred Ministers in these Colonies and be Baptised." [11]

Thus gradually, for the most part imperceptibly, and without the benefit of any synod's advice, the New England churches revamped their policies to make baptism available to all professing Christians of good behavior and to their children. Although this silent revolution effected a change far more drastic than that made by the synod of 1662, and although the vast majority of New England churches probably participated in it, it has understandably received little attention because, during the years it was taking place, a similar but far more spectacular and noisy change was under way in a substantial minority of churches.[12]

The Mathers and probably most other New England ministers, while extending baptism and courting the English Presbyterians, continued to restrict the Lord's Sup-

11. *Ratio Disciplinae Fratrum Nov-Anglorum* (Boston, 1726), p. 80. Cf. Miller, *Colony to Province,* p. 114; Walker, *Creeds and Platforms,* pp. 278–79.

12. But see Walker, *Creeds and Platforms,* pp. 278–79; Miller, *Colony to Province,* pp. 113–14.

per. But there are hints that as early as the 1660's some ministers may have been offering full communion on the same liberal terms that came to prevail for baptism. In 1664 Jonathan Mitchel had advocated the halfway covenant as a means of preserving the restriction of full communion,[13] and three years later he felt obliged to warn that "though Rigid *Severity* in Admissions to the Lords Table is to be avoided; yet to be lax and slight therein, to admit all sorts to full Communion, or upon very slight *Qualifications*, is against the Principles and against the Interest of *Reformation.*" [14]

In 1677 Increase Mather, who had been persuaded by Mitchel's arguments to support the halfway covenant, repeated Mitchel's warning more pointedly. "I wish," he said, "there be not Teachers found in our Israel, that have espoused loose, large Principles here, designing to bring all persons to the Lords Supper, who have an Historical Faith, and are not scandalous in life, although they never had Experience of a work of Regeneration on their Souls." [15]

Probably most New Englanders knew that Mather had in mind the Reverend Solomon Stoddard of Northampton, who in 1677 began to practice what came to be known in New England as open communion, that is, admission of candidates to full membership (including the right to the Lord's Supper) without any attempt to discern saving faith. Stoddard had a high view of his office as minister and declined to direct his efforts exclusively or even mainly toward the nourishment of faith in those who already had

13. *A Defence of the Answer*, pp. 45–46.
14. *Nehemiah on the Wall in Troublesom Times* (Cambridge, 1671), p. 28. This was an election sermon preached in 1667.
15. *A Discourse Concerning the Danger of Apostasy* (election sermon, 1677) in *A Call from Heaven*, p. 84.
16. Miller, *Colony to Province*, pp. 226–36, 269–87.

it. He thought it was impossible anyhow to determine who had faith and who did not; and he threw himself into the conversion of sinners by hellfire sermons that produced a series of religious revivals in Northampton.[16]

In 1679, when a synod convened at Boston to discuss the sins of the land that required reformation, Stoddard and Mather became the principal adversaries in a heated discussion about the terms of communion.[17] The synod decided that no one should be admitted to full communion "without making a personal and publick profession of their Faith and Repentance, either orally, or in some other way, so as shall be to the just satisfaction of the Church." [18] Though Mather later claimed this statement as an endorsement of the old New England way, the wording was equivocal.[19] It could be interpreted to mean that no more than a profession of faith was needed. That the words were intended to allow such an interpretation became apparent when Stoddard disclosed that the synod had refused to authorize an explicit statement advocated by Mather, "That persons should make a Relation of the work of Gods Spirit upon their hearts." [20] It does not follow that the majority of the synod was against such relations, but evidently a majority refused to go on record as requiring them.

After the debate in the synod of 1679, Stoddard did not for some time offer a formal public defense of his views, but it is likely that his practices spread from Northampton to neighboring ministers in the Connecticut Valley. Meanwhile the trend toward a more inclusive church was mov-

17. Walker, *Creeds and Platforms*, p. 419; Solomon Stoddard, *An Appeal to the Learned* (Boston, 1709), p. 93.

18. Walker, *Creeds and Platforms*, p. 433.

19. Increase Mather, *A Dissertation wherein the Strange Doctrine* . . . (Boston, 1708), p. 89.

20. Stoddard, *Appeal to the Learned*, p. 93.

ing in the East too at a rate more rapid than the Mathers could endorse. At Harvard College, from 1685 to 1697, two tutors, William Brattle and John Leverett, encouraged students in a comprehensive view of the church, even recommending Anglican books to them. In 1696 Brattle moved into the pulpit of Jonathan Mitchel's old church in Cambridge and expounded similar views there.[21] The following year, when Cotton Mather published a life of Mitchel, Increase appended a preface, addressed "To the Church at Cambridge in New England and to the Students of the Colledge there." Here Increase sounded again and more urgently the warning he had given twenty years earlier. He set forth at length the views of Mitchel on the necessity of relations of saving grace for all candidates for full membership in the church, and he exhorted the students and the church to remain true to Mitchel's and New England's principles.[22]

In Boston too there were advocates of open communion, and in 1699 with the support of Leverett and Brattle they founded a new church in Brattle Street, with a manifesto defining their principles, which departed from the New England way at a number of points.[23] They thought it proper to baptize all professing Christians and their children (here agreeing with the Mathers). They also maintained that all such persons should have a voice in choosing the pastor. They thought that partakers in the Lord's Supper should be persons of "visible Sanctity," but they left it to the pastor alone, without a church vote, to discern this quality, allowing the candidate to make a relation of religious experiences if he wished to, but not requiring it.

When Increase Mather replied to the challenge of the

21. Walker, *Creeds and Platforms*, p. 472; Miller, *Colony to Province*, pp. 237–38; S. E. Morison, *Harvard College in the Seventeenth Century* (Cambridge, Mass., 1936), pp. 504–507, 541–46.
22. *Ecclesiastes* (Boston, 1697).

new church with a tract reaffirming the importance of relations and of a vote by the church in admission of members, Solomon Stoddard returned to the dispute.[24] By this time Stoddard had become a powerful force in New England ecclesiastical life, a veritable "pope" in the Connecticut Valley. In *The Doctrine of Instituted Churches*,[25] Stoddard swung his whole weight against the conception of the church and of church membership that had prevailed in New England from the beginning. He repudiated the very idea of a gathered church as we have followed it from London and Norwich to Holland and America. Church covenants, he said, were unscriptural. A church was a territorial unit that embraced all professing Christians within it, whether regenerate or unregenerate. Local churches should not be autonomous; they should be subject to ecclesiastical councils composed of ministers. Though he would allow the members of a local church to elect their pastor, he endowed the pastor once elected with powers that reached far beyond those which had been customary in New England: he should not be subject to dismissal by the church and should have sole powers within the church to decide who was fit for the sacraments (but should admit all not scandalous), and with ruling elders he should have sole powers of discipline.

Stoddard's views of church government were Presbyterian, and went beyond the Brattle Street manifesto, at least in the vigor of their expression. They were, however, welcomed by the Brattle Street group, who now declared explicitly that the idea of a church covenant "is a stranger to the Scripture," and that the requirement of a relation of a work of grace was as bad as the requirement of "Oaths,

23. *A Manifesto or Declaration, Set Forth by the Undertakers of the New Church Now Erected in Boston* [Boston, 1699].
24. *The Order of the Gospel* (Boston, 1700).
25. London, 1700.

Subscriptions, and Conformity to a Thousand more Ceremonies." [26] "Wo be to the world," they said, "if all were
to be rated, denyers of Christ, who whether from inability,
modesty or a just indignation, refuse to make a quaint
Speech in the Church." [27]

Few New Englanders were willing to go along with
Stoddard and the Brattle Street group in repudiating the
whole conception of gathered churches, but many, especially in the Connecticut Valley, espoused the opening of
both baptism and the Lord's Supper to professing Christians of good behavior. Samuel Willard, who wrote the
nearest thing to a *Summa Theologica* of New England
Puritanism, came out flatly for open communion and denied that there was any scriptural foundation for the testing of saving faith by relations of religious experience.[28]

By the opening of the eighteenth century, then, New
England Puritans had repudiated in varying degrees the
restriction of church membership adopted in the 1630's.
Some repudiated gathered churches altogether; some,
while retaining church covenants, admitted professing
Christians to all privileges of membership without proof
of saving faith; and probably almost all admitted them to
baptism. Thus in their different ways New Englanders
tempered their zeal and adjusted their churches to a more
worldly purity; and the cycle which began with the gathering of Separatist churches in London and Norwich in
the sixteenth century reached its completion.

But zeal for purity in the church did not die away altogether. In struggling to prevent New Englanders from

26. *Gospel Order Revived* ([New York], 1700), p. 13.
27. *Ibid.*, p. 8.
28. *A Compleat Body of Divinity* (Boston, 1726), p. 863. This work
was the result of a series of sermons preached between 1688 and
1707.

carrying their adjustment to the world too far, Increase Mather predicted in 1700 that if the views exemplified by Stoddard should gain as rapidly in the ensuing thirty years as they had in the preceding thirty, godly people in New England would have to "gather Churches out of churches." [29] Mather did not miss the mark by much.

The ardent preaching of men like Stoddard, who frightened sinners with vivid pictures of hell, was well designed to stir religious zeal. And after Stoddard's death the techniques of hellfire preaching continued to be refined both in England and America, until the whole Atlantic community burst out in the religious revival known in America as the Great Awakening. The zeal engendered by the Awakening among a number of New Englanders produced a new Separatist movement: fired by a vision of their own new purity, converts regarded their old churches as mixed assemblies and broke off to form new churches composed solely of the elect.[30]

At first these self-confessed saints were regarded with as much horror as the Separatists had been in sixteenth-century England. But the new movement for purity gained sudden respectability in 1748 when Jonathan Edwards, the grandson of Solomon Stoddard and Stoddard's successor in the influential pulpit at Northampton, announced that he could no longer admit candidates to full communion without proof of saving grace. The next year, in a treatise defending his view, he denounced not only Stoddardeanism but also the granting of baptism to any but visible saints and their children.[31] In other words, he repudiated

29. *The Order of the Gospel,* p. 12.

30. C. C. Goen, *Revivalism and Separatism in New England, 1740–1800* (New Haven, 1962).

31. *A Humble Inquiry into the Rules of the Word of God, Concerning the Qualifications Requisite to a Complete Standing and Full Communion in the Visible Christian Church* (Boston, 1749).

even the halfway covenant and called for a return to the system established in the 1630's. Edwards possessed the most powerful theological mind of the eighteenth century, and in a series of treatises he was able to furnish a new morphology of conversion adapted to the Lockean psychology of the eighteenth century. When disciples flocked to him and carried his views throughout New England, they launched a new cycle in the history of the idea that we have followed in this study. The new cycle too has long since run its course, which was far different from that of the earlier one. But as long as men strive to approach God through the church, the world will never seem pure enough for the saints, and the Puritan experience will never be wholly unfamiliar.

INDEX

A dultery, 51–52

Ainsworth, Henry: and communion in Amsterdam church, 46–47; splits with F. Johnson, 50; and reinterpretation of Separatist practices, 54–58; and tests of faith, 62, 73, 75; and John Cotton, 103; mentioned, 65, 136

Albigensians, 113

Ames, William: and church covenants, 29; and Separatist principles, 31; and Mass. Puritans, 65; and faith as a mark of the church, 74; and church membership, 77; mentioned, 13, 136, 137

Amsterdam: Separatist churches in, 18; Francis Johnson's church in, 43–44, 46–52; John Smyth's church in, 45; nonseparating English church in, 79–80; John Davenport in, 135–36

Anabaptists: and Donatists, 4; and Calvin, 21; and Separatists, 23, 24; and New England Puritans, 93, 125

Anglican Church: Puritan attack on, 6–16; Puritan practices within, 19–20, 29–32, 74–80; Separatist attack on, 20–32, 54–57; and the means of grace, 116; in Boston, 143

Apocrypha, 6

Arminianism, 136–37

Assurance, 69–70, 91–92

Augustine, Saint, 2–4, 33

B aillie, Robert, 82n., 111–12

Baptism: and Anabaptists, 4; among Separatists, 45–46; in Salem church, 85–86; as means of grace, 121; in New England system, 125–30; and halfway covenant, 130–38; and John Davenport, 135–36; more comprehensive policy of, 143–45

Baptists, 113, 125

Barrow, Henry: and London Separatist church, 18; and Calvin, 23–25; and admission procedures, 38; execution of, 18, 40; and confession of faith, 56; mentioned, 65, 136

Baxter, Richard, 105–106, 124